The Road to American Dreams

The Road to American Dreams:

Mental Health for American Life for Immigrants

Damian Byungsuk Kim, M.D.

VANTAGE PRESS
New York

The opinions expressed herein are solely those of the author.

The author would like to thank The Institute for Korean-American Culture for their help in the preparation of this book.

FIRST EDITION

Published by Vantage Press, Inc.
516 West 34th Street, New York, New York 10001

Manufactured in the United States of America
ISBN: 0-533-14028-5

Library of Congress Catalog Card No.: 01-126764

0 9 8 7 6 5 4 3 2 1

Contents

Preface

All immigrants come to America with dreams. It is good to have dreams, but the road to actualizing these American dreams is not a smooth one at all. Every immigrant needs guidance to proceed on this road. However, none can guide anyone through every step of the process. In this book, I try to provide the guidance about the most important elements of all, the mental attitude and mental health in pursuit of these dreams.

This book is the English version of my recently revised earlier books, titled *Mental Health for American Life,* originally written in Korean. Since its publication in August 1992, this book has swiftly become one of the best-sellers among Korean immigrants. There have been numerous requests from readers to have this book translated into English for their children who can read English only. After seeing many Asian youths suffering from confusion and identity crises, I decided to launch this project hoping to help young immigrants and children of immigrants adjust to America better, lead happier American lives and fulfill their American dreams. This book is intended to help any English-speaking ethnic group beyond Korean-Americans.

According to the US Census of 1990, about 20,000 Koreans immigrated to the United States in that year joining the nearly one million Korean immigrants already living in this country. Different from immigrants arriving in the U.S. before restrictions were lifted in 1965, these more recent immigrants show a broader range of characteristics. They range from those who are "right off the boat" to those already living in the U.S. for 30 years; from those who are struggling to find a means of livelihood to those who have established a sound business; from those who work hard at a fruit/vegetable store to professionals such as doctors, lawyers, and accountants; from those who speak no English to those who use only English; from infants to the elderly in their 70's or 80's; from those who are non-immigrant high school and college students to employees dispatched to branch offices of various corporations and banks or staff the embassy and consul general; first, second, or third generation immigrants; and so on.

What is most interesting to know about this varied group of immigrants is how well they are adjusting to this strange land and culture. As a psychiatrist, I am most interested in this fact because the degree of one's adjustment to this new culture is directly related to the mental health of the individual. In other words, if you can adjust well you will have sound mental health. And, if you have healthier mental status, you can adjust better. Since I came to the United States 36 years ago, I have seen many immigrants who were suffering because of unhealthy mental status. This is an evidence that many immigrants are suffering because of unhealthy mental status. As the result, there are many people who are suffering from personal, family, or children's problems as well as mental illness. To make matters worse, there are few guides to show one how to handle these problems, where and how to seek treatment, or better, how to lead a happier American life.

I receive many calls everyday from Korean immigrants seeking advice for their problems. Every time, I am shocked by the fact that they don't know America, are ignorant about American life, and lack common sense about emotional problems and mental illness. Therefore, I decided to write a guide for these immigrants as well as for future immigrants, students, resident officers of the Foreign Ministry, or resident staff of foreign corporations. My decision was based on my experience of American life as an individual as well as a psychiatrist and psychoanalyst dealing with the mental health and human mind.

I am certain this book will benefit many immigrants especially from Asian countries where Confucianism is the predominant cultural backbone, such as the Far Eastern and some South Eastern countries.

Although many examples and observations are based on Asians, especially Koreans, most of it can be applied to immigrants of any ethnic group. The definition of Asian is very broad. In this book, it mainly refers to the three Far Eastern countries namely China, Japan, Korea, and some other Asian countries heavily influenced by Confucianism.

On the other hand, this book will also help non-immigrant Americans understand some aspects of the culture, customs, thoughts, and expectations of immigrants.

I hope this book will fulfill what it intends to as well as one of my own American dreams.

The Road to American Dreams

I

Immigration and the Beginning of Troubles

Legal immigration of Koreans to the United States began in 1903. Prior to this, in May 1882, *The Treaty of Korean-American Friendship and Trade* was signed. On September 2, 1883, a goodwill envoy led by Yong-Shik Min landed in San Francisco, California. One of the envoys, Kil-June Yu, stayed on in the United States to study. He later returned to Korea through Europe and published a book titled, *What I Saw and Heard in the West*, which was the first book introducing the West and Western Culture through the perspective of a Korean's experience. In 1885, Jae-Pil Suh took political refuge in the U.S. with two other people. Then in 1892, he became the first Korean born medical doctor educated in the United States. For the first 2 years after legalization of immigration in 1903, about 7,000 Korean men entered Hawaii as laborers. Americans praised the Korean laborers as the most gentle and hard working of all Asians who came to the United States.

The period between 1905 and 1941 was the time when some immigrants took political asylum in the United States from Japanese rule and some students entered the country for advanced education. After the end of the Second World War in 1945, there was only restricted entry to the United States for some students and diplomats. Prior to 1963, the

1

United States limited the numbers of immigrants from specific countries or ethnic groups from entering the country under the Quarter System. After the immigration law was revised in 1965 and the Quarter System was repealed, mass immigration of Koreans to the United States began.

Dr. Jae-Pil Suh, who took political refuge in 1885, wrote in the diaries, " ... We do not speak English, do not know anyone and do not have any money. Nobody pays any attention to us. We feel like poor, lonely orphans thrown out of the ship which carried us across the Pacific Ocean. . . ." What a sad, lonely, heartbreaking scream it is! In these words, there are many issues that may damage mental health and induce mental illness. About one century has passed since his experience. Has there been any change? Are things any different today?

II
What Does Mental Health Mean?

The words "mental health" only mean the status of the mind or psyche in terms of how healthy it is. Therefore, it could be healthy or unhealthy. When one speaks of healthy mental state, in brief it means that you sleep well, eat well, work well, get along well with your family and others, and live with a peaceful mind. This seems simple enough. But, you have to have *all of these consistently while not missing a single one.* When we say mental health, it usually refers to maintaining a healthy mental state. This is broken into two conditions. First, when you already have a healthy mental state you must prevent its deterioration. Second, when you have emotional suffering or mental disease, you must return to the previous healthy state through appropriate treatment.

Healthy mental status is not an issue limited to the individual. It is closely and directly connected to one's physical health, family life, occupational life, social life, school life and how these factors are affecting each other. Now, let us examine each one of these in relationship to mental health.

1. Physical Health

As the well-known expression states "sound body, sound mind," physical health is important for a healthy mental state. Of course, if you have a weak body or are suffering from chronic disease, your mind cannot be comfortable. However, as we know, we don't have much control over physical illness. You just go to the family doctor or to a specialist and leave the treatment to them. In contrast to physical illness, many mental problems can be prevented if you deal with them at an early stage. But even if you do go to a psychiatrist, you cannot leave everything to him. You have to cooperate with the psychiatrist by opening up with what you think or feel without holding back. If you keep unresolved emotional problems suppressed for a while, you may develop symptoms of physical disease although you don't actually have the disease.

When you have actual physical disease, the condition can either improve quickly or become worse, depending on your state of mind. For example, without any obvious physical reasons one can suffer from severe headaches, indigestion, epigastric burning, joint pain, palpitations, shortness of breath, insomnia, loss of appetite, etc. In contrast to these symptoms, with actual physical disease such as angina, stomach ulcer, colitis, asthma, and high blood pressure, emotional factors play a major role in their production. Therefore, for the treatment of these diseases maintaining a peaceful mind is essential.

One of the characteristics of people in general is that they develop various physical disease symptoms from emotional problems although they don't have an actual physical illness. This phenomenon is called "somatization of mental problems." This phenomenon has a lot to do with ethnicity and its culture, and it is common throughout many Asian countries. Actually, it can be seen in both the East and West when emotional conflict lasts a long time. But, this somatization phenomenon with Asians, especially Koreans, complicates the mental health problem because it can prolong the suffering and prevent the sufferer from obtaining psychiatric treatment in time. This is due in part to the physician's reluctance to refer the patient to a psychiatrist, and/or the denial of emotional problems on the part of the individual. At any rate, one must remember that when one's state of mind is unhealthy one can develop physical symptoms or physical illness. It is true to state "sound body, sound mind," but the reverse is also just as true: "sound mind, sound body."

2. Family Lives and Mental Health

If you don't have a healthy mind, your family life can't be peaceful either. Naturally, your spouse, relatives or children may create problems, but what I would like to explore is how your own state of mind affects your family life. If the state of one's mind is healthy, one can easily handle many problems that may occur at home and can live in harmony with one's family, relatives and parents. However, if the state of your mind is unhealthy and not peaceful, it can cause the breakdown of harmony within the family unit. I am referring to those people who are irritable, annoying to their family, and argumentative with their spouses. Moreover, some look for temporary solutions to their emotional problems by drinking alcohol or by having extra-marital affairs that complicate their family problems.

There was a man who made a good amount of money by running a store in a dangerous neighborhood. He sold the store in order to relocate his business to a safer neighborhood. However, he was not able to find another business for several months. He began to feel nervous and was unable to cope with the stress of not being able to find a new business quickly and from living on the shrinking funds he had made from selling the old store. He became cranky at home, lost his temper without provocation, began to drink heavily, and eventually started having an affair with a hostess he met in a bar. As a result, there were frequent arguments between the man and his wife with each one threatening the other with divorce. Finally, his parents and older brother persuaded the man to seek psychiatric help and he was referred to me. After a course of treatment, he understood that he was acting on his anxiety, and his irritable behavior subsided. This is only one example to illustrate how an unhealthy mind can affect a person's family life adversely, but there are many similar cases.

3. Occupational Life

When your mind is healthy and peaceful, you can carry out most difficult tasks with ease. You are more able to get along well with your supervisor and your co-workers. Of course, it is obvious that your job performance will be affected if your mind is not healthy.

A staff member working at the branch office of a giant Korean company sought psychiatric treatment, complaining of anxiety, palpitations, and poor concentration at work. He revealed that he had been in the United States for three years, and he had to return to his main office in Korea in six months. For the sake of his children's education, his wife and two children would stay here in the United States for a while. But as a result of preparing to make these changes in his life, he became nervous, unable to carry out his work, and unable to sleep well at night. At first glance, it seemed like he couldn't function well at his job because of the external factors. On the contrary, it should be viewed as a problem stemming from, and beginning with, his unhealthy mental state.

4. Social Life

Man can't live in isolation from other humans. People are social creatures and we live in close relationship to others. If I have a healthy mental status, my relationship with others will be pleasurable and it will be rewarding to be compassionate with one another; whereas, if my mental condition is unhealthy, it will be more stressful to have relationships with others—while at the same time living alone may also be stressful. In addition, I may try to take my frustrations out on others, which in turn leads to rejection by those others. As we all know, if one has a mental illness it is difficult or impossible to establish successful relationships with others.

There was a young man who sought psychiatric treatment at my office complaining of depression and an inability to make friends. In the course of treatment, it became apparent that he had a severe inferiority complex. In order to get over it, he had been behaving so badly that no one liked him. Unaware of his actions, he ridiculed, slandered, and twisted the words of others. He was a quiet, introverted man who had grown up in Korea and he had managed to get along fairly well with his friends prior to coming to the United States. However, after immigrating to America his inferiority complex worsened, due to the racial discrimination he had to endure. As a result, his unconscious efforts to get over his inferiority complex backfired and his interpersonal relationships became sour. Eventually, he was unable to tolerate the pain of being lonely.

5. School Life

School life is one of the most important grounds on which to broaden knowledge and cultivate emotion. As we all know, in order to study well, it is necessary to have high concentration power. However, if one's mind is not peaceful—that is, if one's mental status is not healthy, one cannot concentrate. If a student who is affected by anxiety, depression, and homesickness is sitting in the classroom thinking about the scene of his parents' fight, or thinking about the frustrations he had because of communication problems, or frictions he may have with other students, how will he be able to study well?

School life has a profound relationship with mental health for both the children of immigrants and those who come to study in America. If the student adjusts to the immigrants' life quickly and maintains healthy mental conditions, he will have smooth relationships with other students, concentrate well in his studies, and enjoy school life thoroughly. However, if his adaptation is unwholesome or incomplete, he will become cranky, negative passive, and neurotic and create many other accompanying problems. Finally, he may start to look for other more rewarding activities or relationships outside of school and become an extremely troubled child. This is one of the major reasons why I object to sending children abroad to study early, before college age, because that is the period when children go through emotional maturation, character formation, and individual identity establishment. Those who come here after high school graduation must also try to maintain their mental health in order to achieve their academic goals.

I have met many parents who claim that the main purpose of their immigration to America is for better education of their children. If that is truly the case, they should pay more attention to their mental health and emotional growth.

We briefly reviewed the relationship between mental health and an individual's physical health, family life, social life, and school life. We can cite an example of one so-called insane person who disrupted the entire world; that is the cruel political dictator, Adolf Hitler. Such harsh, inhumane religious and political leaders are not difficult to find throughout the course of human history.

In this book, I am going to deal with the subject of an individual's mental health in relationship to his or her personal life. In our lives, it is inevitable to encounter external stress and conflicts stemming from family life, one's occupation, and interpersonal relationships. What causes these stresses can be divided into two categories. First, problems derived from external factors. And, second, problems that stem from internal factors; meaning that "I, myself, am the cause of the problem." The former occurs when the problems are caused by external factors such as your job, family, school, society, a natural disaster, etc. These will cause emotional stress or personal problems which if not handled appropriately may lead to a mental disorder. However, if you have a sound mental condition, you can manage the external and internal factors more adequately to resolve those problems and prevent the onset of mental illness. Also, if you lead your life with a healthy mind you can prevent family, on-the-job, school, or social problems that may develop because of you, yourself. Whereas, there are many factors that can cause mental stress in the life of immigrants. There are many additional problems due to the fact that most immigrants do not have any time to address those stresses.

As stated above, when one speaks of mental health it is not only with regard to an individual's specific problem, but it also involves one's physical health, family, occupation, social life, and school. Therefore, when dealing with an individual's mental health, you must also look at the overall issues associated with that person.

III

Characteristics of American Life and the Problems That Immigrants Experience

The problems of mental health can occur to *any*one, *any*where, and *any*time regardless of whether or not it is the aftermath of immigration. However, the reason that I try to focus on the mental problems of immigration life is because there are characteristic aspects of immigration life and many sources of stress that are different from those of living in one's country of origin. Therefore, it frequently becomes a survival issue to maintain a healthy mental state in order to lead a successful American life. For example, if you did not immigrate to America, then you would not have to suffer from the problems of communicating in English. You would not have to become furious over racial prejudice, and you would not have to put yourself in embarrassing situations for not knowing the American culture and customs. Now, let us review some of the characteristics and problems of immigration life.

1. Re-rooting in America

Immigration is like transplanting a full-grown tree; uprooting it intact, moving it somewhere else with different soil, planting it, and helping it to lay roots again. This is different from raising a seedling because the transplanted tree has to lay roots quickly and strongly; otherwise it may fall down or wither away. Therefore, the stress of immigration is much greater than moving a household in one's own country. First of all, you need to find a place to live. However, it's not an easy task to decide in which town or city to live in this large land. You also must decide how you will make a living. Most immigrants are not professionals, and even if you are one, you won't be able to work as a professional in the United States until you obtain the proper license to do so. Also, most people do not immigrate with a lot of funds. Therefore, your finances will be tight. It is common to see many immigrant families living on limited funds anxiously looking for months (and, at times, years) for a business to start. Moreover, for those who had solid businesses or replete financial means in their country of origin the stress is tremendous. For this reason, many immigrant families live temporarily in ethnic areas such as Flushing, Queens, in New York City, and then move to the surrounding suburbs as they become more stable. Also, many change their businesses a few times. In the beginning, they start fruit and vegetable markets that are easier to build up through hard work. Then, they change to an easier business such as dry cleaning. However, it is rare to own a business compatible with your education or specialty. There is a tendency to consider making a living and accumulating savings as the priority. As a result, there are many families where the husband and wife both work in a business which demands hard physical labor, is dangerous and beneath his or her qualifications. According to a recent newspaper article, Asians run most of the retail businesses in the New York area. The popular businesses for Korean immigrants are: fruit and vegetable stores, fish markets, shoe-repair shops, dry cleaners, deli stores, grocery stores, variety stores, stationery shops, and similar businesses. Korean women monopolize ownership of the nail salons and massage parlors. Because it is so urgent to have something to eat, many Korean immigrants engage in the hardest working businesses regardless of their education or social class in Korea. Therefore, it is inevitable to develop secondary problems with their children stemming from neglect or from not giving them enough affection or from an injured pride due to engaging in a job considered to be lower than one's capabilities. These stresses will eventually lead one to mental health problems.

2. Lacking a "Sense of Being the Host"

Immigration may mean leaving your native land, country, and compatriots to go and live with other ethnic groups in a strange land seeking a better life. Therefore, immigrants can't avoid feeling like tenants or tourists and can't have the sense of being the host of the land or the country. The tenant can't become the landlord no matter how rich he grows unless he leaves the apartment. If the hosts look like us, use the same language, have the same customs, and think along the same lines, after a few years we may feel like we're living in our native country. But, that is not the case when we immigrate to America. Of course, legally, we can live in this country permanently or become naturalized citizens. However, it is only a legal status and can't change our feelings.

Many of those who came to this land ahead of us do not let other ethnic groups who are following them feel at home, or rather reject them. When we Asians join whites or blacks at a party or conference, they sometimes ask where we are from. If you say you are from New York, their facial expression turns sour and they don't try to continue the conversation. This is probably because they can't comprehend how a moon-faced, yellow-skinned person can say New York or the United States is his or her native land. Of course, what they want to know is which country you are from originally. If, after noticing the uncomfortable feeling you have stirred up in them, you say you are originally from Korea they usually become relaxed and continue chatting with you. After having a few similar experiences, I now avoid an uncomfortable situation by telling them in a breath that I originally came from Korea and am now living in New York. The one and a half generations in America may say the same. But, what about the second generation, those who are born in America? Will they say, "My parents are from Korea but I was born in New York" with a sense of apology—or with pride?

Until a few years ago, some Americans asked me occasionally when I was planning to return to my native country. But, this is rare now in a big metropolitan area. Judging from all these experiences, one can assume that many Americans do not accept Asians as one of the hosts of this country like themselves, but as tourists, tenants, or temporary residents. I have lived in this country for 35 years, but I still do not have the feeling of being one of the hosts of this country. In my observation, many immigrants do not have close relationships outside their own ethnic group. Typically, their association is for business matters and not based on mutual affection. As a result, most immigrants live closely with their own genre. Possibly, the immigrant generation can never be able to feel they are one of the hosts of this land no matter how long they live in this country, although legally or intellectually they may belong. This poor sense of being the host of this country will interfere with the immigrant's ability to live with high spirits and adjust to this society. So, why did we come to live in America if we do not feel rightful or equitable? Or, why don't we return to the country of origin if we have achieved the goals we intended by coming to America? And, why do you want to live in this country when you don't have the feeling of being the host of this land and of being equal?

3. Living in Three Different Cultures

All immigrants commonly think that they are living in two cultures; the native culture they came with and the culture of the host land. This is the case in the beginning of the immigrant life, and while there are only a small number of immigrants. However, it is not the case as their lives in this land become longer and the numbers in the same ethnic group multiply. Gradually, they begin to create a new culture that is neither purely their original culture nor purely the host land's culture. It is a mixture or a compromise of these two cultures. This is the third culture they will also be living in. Before going any further, let us give some thought to what happens to the native culture that immigrants bring with them to America.

A. Melting Pot, Mosaic, Salad Bowl, or Rainbow?

In the past, the understanding of American scholars was that the original or native culture that immigrants bring with them would melt away in the big melting pot of American culture and disappear. This may have been the case when most immigrants were from Europe and ethnically white. This phenomenon has never created any problem and they never questioned it then. However, things have changed over the years due to the increased number of non-white ethnic immigrants.

The "American Melting Pot" is no longer big enough or strong enough to melt away all these different ethnic cultures.

Now, the new philosophy is the co-existence of all these distinctive cultures. The analogies are that it's like a mosaic, a rainbow, or a bowl of salad. The reasons behind this change are not only because the American Melting Pot isn't strong enough or big enough, but based on the realization that there is so much all these different cultures can add to enrich the American culture, which is arguably not the world's best culture. All these ethnic groups function poorly when they lose their original identity. And, when they maintain their original culture, they boost their pride and dignity; they function better and contribute much more to American society.

B. The Third Culture

The fusing of the immigrant's original culture with American culture is destined to create a new culture. Of course, some elements of the culture remain—as in a salad—but overall it is different from simply a "bowl of salad." The analogy may be the border zone between two adjoining colors of a rainbow. This is a blend of two colors different from both of the original colors. Most of us are unconscious or unaware of these blends, or do not talk about them, but they exist and bond the two colors. Likewise, the newly created third culture plays the important role of initially bonding two cultures, and then gradually expanding into the territories of the original two. As the immigrant generation advances, children of immigrants will mostly live in this new culture. Therefore, I can't overemphasize the importance of this new culture and the efforts that contemporary immigrants must make to help this third culture develop healthy, strong, and morally acceptable denizens. After all, our children will continue to live in America and to live in this very new culture.

4. America Is "The Land of Opportunity"

What is meant by the phrase "The Land of Opportunity"? This means having access to the highest opportunity to study and research in every field, to enjoy political and religious freedom, to bring one's artistic creativity into full play, to run a business as one wishes, to earn wealth, to actualize one's idea or invention, to raise and educate one's children in a freer and more comfortable atmosphere, to receive the benefits of a social welfare system, even to enjoy playing golf without much financial strain or stretching the rights of peddlers to beg. The opportunities are endless. This is, in fact, because the United States covers a huge land area, is highly populated, and is a land where people from all over the world gather to live. The speed of new development is so fast that abundant opportunities are being created continuously. Therefore, the society is structured in such a way as to help you actualize your potential and pursue your dream goals if you are motivated and diligent. Even if you are in the minority, people will support you fully if you are considered to be useful.

For Koreans and Korean Americans, one of the most significant opportunities in America is to introduce Korea and the Orient, that is, Oriental thinking, philosophy, culture, history, religion, arts, humanity—to American culture. Such opportunities are ample because many Americans are looking for a way out of economic disappointment and social ills through Oriental philosophy and culture. Another important opportunity is to attempt the grafting of Western and Eastern culture. Because it means a creation of a new culture, the opportunity will be endlessly abundant. For all these reasons, America is the wide open "Land of Opportunity" where progressive, adventurous, and creative immigrants should challenge. This can be one of the answers to the question raised in the previous chapter. "Why do you want to live in this country when you don't have the feeling of being the host of this land and of being equal?"

IV
Problems with Adjustment

Adjustment refers to the process of yielding oneself to the environment. Therefore, it refers to the passive process in which the environment remains the same while the human being must accommodate to the environment. It is the process before men become active. This chapter examines offering aspects of adjustment. Because people must abandon or modify their natural way of life and customs that they are already accustomed to in one environment and develop a new way of life and customs in another environment, it is inevitable to encounter difficulties and problems in the process of acculturation.

1. The Communication Problem

There are two reasons for communication difficulty among Korean immigrants and Americans.

A. Not Enough Everyday Conversational English

What an inconvenience it is that Americans don't understand the fluent Korean that you are used to, and your English isn't as fluent as your Korean. You can't make or receive a telephone call properly. You may have a hard time with shopping. At times, your children's school principal or teacher may want to see you and you'll want to know the reason; but it's not clear from what your children tell you. Yet, you are afraid to discuss it over the telephone because of your poor English let alone going to school to face these authorities. So, you give up or ignore the request. In another situation, you may go to the hospital emergency room for a medical emergency. But, due to poor communication with the doctors and nurses you may not get the appropriate care that is needed.

In fact, even if you are a college graduate who excelled at the English language in school in Korea, you will have a lot of difficulty communicating in English here in America unless you learned English conversation separately and extensively for a few years. The reason is because what you studied in school was mostly English grammar and writings but not everyday, conversational English. It is a known fact that English language education in Korea is academic rather than pragmatic. But fortunately, the Korean government finally came to the realization of this fact and has recently changed the curriculum, placing more emphasis on English conversation and starting it in elementary school. This will benefit the next generation of Korean youth.

When it comes to communication problems, even I am not an exception. Although I was one of the "A" students in English throughout high school and college, I encountered a great deal of difficulty with communication in America resulting in many comic episodes due to my poor everyday English. My first year in the United States was spent as a medical intern at the Rochester General Hospital in Rochester, New York. When I was on call at night, I became frustrated whenever a nurse from the ward called me because I couldn't understand her clearly. However, realizing that things could become worse if I stayed on the telephone and tried to figure out what she wanted, I used to ask her what ward she was calling me from and I ran to that floor. Of course, it was a nuisance to get out of bed in the middle of the night! However, my reasoning was that it would be easier to figure out what she wanted by communicating face to face than by telephone.

I continued this practice until I gained a better understanding of the new language. As a result, I earned the reputation of being the most sincere, caring, and hard-working intern in the hospital because the nurses did not know what was really going on. Naturally, they preferred me to other American house doctors who tried to handle problems over the telephone even when, in the end, they had to go down to the floor. Many years later, I had chances to meet my Korean medical school classmates and we laughed about the fiascoes we had in the process of adjusting to America. I learned that I was not the only one who had those experiences as an intern!

This is only one example of many interesting experiences I have had in America. What I've learned about the new language is that most conversational English consists of easy, basic words that have various meanings. It takes a long time to grasp the usage of such simple words and idioms. Again, when I was working as an intern, I was assisting the attending surgeon in the operating room. My job was to pull the retractor in order to keep the abdomen surgically open. There were two other doctors and a couple of nurses in the room. The surgeon liked to joke while operating on a patient. I've forgotten what the situation was, but he asked me a question and I answered him.

Then he said, "Don't pull my leg, Doctor!" I became puzzled and replied, "No, I did not pull your leg. I didn't even touch you!"

It took a while for me to learn the idiomatic meaning of "pulling one's leg." I still smile whenever I think of that episode.

B. Communication Problems Due to Cultural Differences

It is expected that there will be differences between Koreans and Americans in expressing feelings or ideas, due to culture. Americans are educated and raised to verbally express their feelings and ideas without hesitation. Therefore, they expect everybody to behave likewise. In contrast, Koreans grow up learning to talk less, and it is a virtue not to express one's feelings or ideas so straightforwardly. As a result, a Korean will try to avoid talking about matters that may result in his own or another's embarrassment as well as matters that are mutually uncomfortable. Instead, Koreans resort to non-verbal communication methods. For example, instead of saying "yes" or "no" clearly, a Korean may try to convey it by means of a facial expression, gesture, smile, wink, cough, light pinching, etc. In addition, he expects the other person to grasp his intention and act on it. Of course, this may or may not work every time, even between Koreans; and it is out of the question between a Korean and an American. Not only does it not work, but may create a misunderstanding or may invite the American to take him as a fool. Americans do not accept anything unless it is expressed verbally or, even better, in writing.

One good example is that of the typical American married couple each of whom must say "I love you" to each other a dozen times a day to convince his or her spouse that he or she really loves him or her. For Koreans, exchanging a loving glance is good enough. So, one may refer to American culture as a verbal culture. What is interesting is that in Korea people respect a quiet person as knowledgeable, scholarly, discreet, and gentle. However, to Americans, this person may appear to be dumb, angry, ignorant, insecure, anti-social, or even guilty. What a contrast! Therefore, many Korean-Americans suffer as the result of poor communication or difficulty in communicating with Americans. Some even receive unfair treatment, if not actual mistreatment. At times, Korean language newspapers report that some Korean-American drivers have been subject to paying compensation when another driver hit their cars because of communication problems. There was an incident in which a Korean-American man captured a mugger who tried to snatch his wallet. When the police arrived, the Korean man was arrested for unproven violence against the mugger. Communication problems due to poor English must be a source of many stresses that many immigrants experience firsthand in the early stages of their American life.

2. The Difference in Customs

As with the differences in appearance, Americans have customs different from those of Koreans. One of the most contrasting examples is in the way men treat women. For Korean men, the idea of a woman walking one step behind her husband still lingers on in their minds. As a result, he tries to dominate women even after immigrating to America. However, in America, men escort women gently and give way to them in many instances. Men may belittle them inside, but externally they are expected to treat women respectfully. This is a custom dating back to the days of chivalry and European knighthood. For example, when getting in the car, entering the house, or in and out of the elevator, men give way to women. This is analogous to the manner in which the youth treat elderly people in Korea. If a man doesn't show respect toward women, he may be called a "barbarian." Well, actually, one can often label other people as barbarians if their behavior is different from one's own.

Another common example is that Americans are accustomed to carrying on conversations at the meal table. In contrast, Koreans are raised not to open their mouths except for eating and this is frequently misunderstood by Americans to mean that a Korean is angry or that he dislikes them or the food.

Actually, what Americans chat about at the table is usually mundane small talk. When I first came to America, I couldn't taste what I was eating and developed indigestion after my meals because I tried so hard to keep up with the conversation in my broken English. When I was doing my internship at Rochester General Hospital, my first year of American life was difficult because of the hard work, my loss of appetite and my inability to adjust quickly to American foods. One morning after working hard on the night shift, I went to eat breakfast at the staff cafeteria. I was so exhausted that I didn't feel like eating anything. However, I did feel that I could swallow cool ice cream. So, I asked for a portion from the woman who was serving foods.

Well, I don't know what she had against me, but she gave me hell with a ridicule; "Do you eat ice cream for breakfast in *your* country?! Not in America! Come back at lunch time!"

I felt so embarrassed that I could have crawled into a hole. I took it as a racial as well as a cultural insult. This is the price we have to pay for trying to live in a dominant and different culture!

I will share another example. The Korean language newspaper has reported incidents similar to this from time to time. In Korea, it is a customarily accepted behavior for adults, especially elderly people, to stroke a male baby's penis as a gesture of saying he is "cute." Therefore, at times in the United States, elderly people who were babysitting for their grandchildren were reported by their American neighbors and arrested for sexual abuse of their grandchildren.

To many Americans it is rude behavior to take off your shoes in front of other people except at places like the beach or swimming pool. So, they keep their shoes on all day, inside as well as outside the house. On the other hand, Koreans love to take off their shoes in any place and at any time. Whether or not it disperses foul odors, you must take off your shoes before entering the room. (In fact, the Korean custom is more sanitary.) But, no matter, if you live in America you must pay attention to American customs.

There are many such differences in everyday customs between the two cultures that cause many newcomers to America to be surprised or dismayed and make them feel nervous or uncomfortable. Cultures and customs have evolved and been followed by different races and ethnic groups throughout their history. No one can say which is good or bad; right or wrong; better or worse. However, in my opinion, it is desirable to respect and follow American customs if you are living in America. Also, it is desirable, when an American is invited to your Korean household, to explain your Korean customs and lead him to follow the Korean way while in your home.

3. The Difference of Value and Worth

America is widely considered to be the country best representative of *capitalism*. In short, is an economic system under which private assets are recognized and free competition

of business is permitted. Therefore, in this society, most people are striving for an affluent material life by "hard work
and ingenuity." In other words, this is a society where you
can sense the dictum "Money is Power." Since the Second
World War, Korea has been ranked as one of the capitalist
countries. However, due to the fact that the history of capitalism in Korea is short and there are deep-rooted, uniquely
Korean values, many Korean immigrants experience dismay
over the difference in values between the two countries. I will
illustrate some examples.

A. "Money Is Number One"

It is a fact that without money you can't have the necessities of life in any country under any political or economic
system. However, there are few other societies on earth where
the arrogance of money has pushed out the dignity of humanity. No matter how attractive you are, how smart you are,
or whether you have a brilliant educational background, or
whether your behavior is honest and clean; if you don't make
enough money, you are trivial and will be pushed aside. To
the contrary, no matter how ugly looking you are, uneducated you are, or whether you commit an abhorrent, immoral
crime; if you make a huge amount of money (regardless of
the means) without being caught, then people will kowtow
to you and you can become a well-respected person.

One good example is the so-called "Crime Family," a
unique product of America. I have no way of knowing who
they are, but according to hearsay, books, and "Godfather"
movies, these people live extravagantly while becoming rich
through cruel and heinous means. Their neighbors and even
the police know that they belong to the "Crime Family."
However, using their wealth as a device, they are not only

able to slip through the legal net but at times they become the subjects of envy and respect.

At any rate, the yardstick of human existence is often determined by how much wealth you possess. America is a democratic country where, theoretically, every human being is equal. That may be declared so in the United States Constitution, but not so in front of money. In reality, if you don't have enough money, you will not be able to enjoy the legal protection of "equal rights." The rich and the children of the rich can get away with not being sent to jail after committing a felony or even murder. But, the poor and the children of the poor are severely punished for crimes of a similar degree. For example, John Hinckley who attempted the assassination of President Reagan, and Robert Chambers who murdered his girlfriend. Both escaped punishment by the manipulation of hyperbolic lawyers their parents had hired. Aside from the truth of whether O.J. Simpson murdered his wife or not, the world witnessed vividly what money can do for the suspected murderer.

Again, it appears that there shouldn't be any social class in American society. However, there are *several* social classes, depending on a person's wealth; ranging from the homeless to the homebound billionaire. Usually, those who belong to a similar class befriend each other and reject or look down on those who are in lower economic classes. I hear about many Korean-American families who want to buy a house in a nice neighborhood as quickly as possible. One man worked very hard day and night and saved enough money to buy a new house. However, he did not yet have enough money to buy a new luxury car. So, he had to leave his old, crummy car in the driveway.

No one in the neighborhood came to welcome him.

One day, a few people knocked on his door and berated him, saying that his old car did not belong in that neighborhood and that he should replace it with a new luxury car—otherwise the prices of houses in the neighborhood would be devalued. In another wealthy neighborhood, when the owner of the houses cuts the grass and does the gardening work, his neighbors pressure him in various ways to hire a gardener to do the work.

So, you have to know how to spend money appropriately according to your social class. Having money is one thing, and knowing how to spend money is another. That is, this is a society where your human value is often determined by the level of your wealth. As a result, there is an overwhelming trend toward trying to accumulate wealth by any means possible—even by sacrificing your self-esteem and pride as a human, or by murdering another human being. As a consequence, there is no other country on earth where there are more thieves, robbers, drug dealers, and murderers than in the United States. In recent days this type of "gold worshiping" has contaminated Korea and there have been occasional reports of shocking crimes in Korea that make American criminality pale by comparison. However, the extent of such crime is not yet as widespread there. But when Koreans immigrate to America, they witness or experience this crime wave personally, or actually become the victims of such crime, and they just feel numb for a while. Since one of the reasons that many immigrants want to live in the New World is to accumulate more material wealth, they quickly become accustomed to this way of life. By which, I do not mean that they would necessarily do anything immoral or criminal. I simply mean there are many immigrants working hard day and night to save up money while pushing everything else aside and becoming voluntary slaves to materialism.

B. Hedonism

Hedonism goes hand in hand with "gold worshiping." Therefore, it is expected that the "gold worshipers" of America will be extravagant in pursuit of all kinds of pleasure. As a result, America is the biggest consumer market in the world; it is the center of luxurious goods, and there is nothing you can't buy or can't do with enough money. There are plenty of goods produced domestically or imported from all over the world. There are valuable gems and opulent items that you never dreamed of seeing in Korea. In America, you can obtain and enjoy them if you have enough money.

Another interesting side of American society is that if you don't have enough money, you can still get by according to your means because there are many different levels of the same kinds of products. For example, there are men's suits ranging in price from fifty dollars to thousands of dollars. So, when you are not making enough money you can live with cheap stuff. But, since there is no cap for human desire, you can hardly suppress the impulse to make a lot of money and buy more expensive, luxurious items. The same applies for pleasure-seeking behavior; if you have a lot of money, all the conditions are ready for you to live like a prince. There are palatial houses with unimaginable gadgets, luxurious limousines, luxurious private airplanes, luxurious private yachts, delicious meals, attractive women, etc. There is nothing you can't obtain or you can't do for pleasure. One billionaire, Malcolm Forbes, reportedly hosted his own birthday party a few years ago spending 3 million dollars, and the self-made millionaire Donald Trump reportedly had to reduce his monthly expenses to $400,000 when he encountered financial trouble several years ago. For ordinary people, the extent of the luxury the super rich enjoy is beyond imagination. Therefore, it's understandable that many immigrants who were not well-to-do in their country of origin become excited and stimulated after seeing all the luxury in America. However, we should remember that in a hedonistic and materialistic society, there is rampant corruption and crime. Because of this, many newly immigrated people become the victims of such predators; that is, mugging, robbery, murder, etc. Also, sex becomes only a means of peripheral pleasure and not of genuine love.

Korea has become economically advanced and richer. Judging from Korean newspapers, there are many extreme incidents and occurrences resulting from the import of the negative products of American capitalism, such as "gold worshiping," hedonism, corruption, and crime. It is an undesirable development, to which the Korean government and society must pay close attention in order to prevent any wide spreading of such malady.

The Koreans in Korea have invented a unique pleasure called the "body nurturing pilgrimage." No other ethnic group on this earth has so many things to promote one's physical health, and for this purpose they will spend more lavishly. You can't help but laugh to hear that many Koreans travel the country and go overseas in groups like a procession of pilgrims looking for the stuff to stuff their stomachs with that are claimed to be good for your health, and spending so much money without hesitation. Not too long ago, a Korean newspaper reported that many Koreans go to Thailand to drink raw cobra's blood because it is claimed to be good for sexual libido. Some of these people come home afflicted by a rare disease that is very difficult to treat. Anyway, my story became sidetracked, but the point I am trying to make is that even though you are accustomed to this type of pleasure in Korea, it's no comparison to American-style hedonism and you will have a hard time digesting and adjusting to it.

C. Individualism

Individualism is defined in *Webster's New World Dictionary* as the leading of one's life in one's own way without regard for others. The individual is the smallest unit that makes up the society; the rights and sovereignty of the individual are respected in individualism. If the issue is not a matter of direct interest to you, you don't get involved. On the other hand, you don't want others to interfere with your matters if they are not matters concerning them. However, individualism has to be differentiated from *selfishness;* that is when you pursue your own interests alone whether you hurt others or not. For Koreans who are accustomed to a family-oriented culture based on Confucianism, individualism impresses them as very cold and inhumane at times. They need time to adjust to American society where individualism prevails. I will list some examples of such differences. The American way of writing your name is your given name first followed by your family name. Koreans write their family name first with the given name after the family name. This eloquently tells you which comes first in the society; the individual or the family.

I've seen some American parents and their mature children buy and sell goods between them. This is something you would seldom find in Korean families. Koreans are not accustomed to a give-and-take way of thinking, where you expect others to pay you back if you do them any favors and you feel obliged to pay them back if you receive any favors. The Good Samaritan attitude is as hard to see in America as it is in Korea. Some extreme examples are incidents reported through the mass media in which people refused to come to the aid of others who are being beaten to death on the street or in the house while screaming for help.

In Korea, it is customary to have three generations living harmoniously in one household. However, in America, it is customary for married children to move out of their parents' house at the time of, or even before, marriage. After the import of capitalism into Korea, the individualistic attitude started to spread little by little and gradually the Korean way of having a "humane" attitude may disappear. No matter how individualistic you have become in Korea, you will be shocked and disappointed to see the extremes of American individualism after immigrating to the United States. In America, the boundaries of personal space between individuals are clear-cut, and you are not supposed to violate these boundaries. However in Korea, these boundaries are often fuzzy and there are problems stemming from this. In Korea, people may bump into each other while passing by but they just continue on their way as if nothing had happened. (Of course, no one apologizes to anyone.) But, in America, people are quick to apologize if they touch the sleeves of each other, or even before touching each other, or better yet when another person bumps into you and clearly the other person is to blame. At first, I felt embarrassed when I stepped on another person's toes and he apologized to me. I even thought he was a hypocrite. It took me many years before I was able to say, "Excuse me!" to the other person in these situations as quickly as he. Anyway, American etiquette is different from what Koreans are accustomed to. This stems from the American's strict way of thinking that you should not invade the "personal space" or boundary between you and others.

D. Only the Tangibles and Visible Are Counted

This attitude stems from materialism, gold worshiping, and hedonism. An episode between Alexander the Great and the philosopher, Diogenes, of ancient Greece is a markedly contrasting one. The story is that one sunny day, Alexander the Great went to see the famous philosopher who was living on the street in a big barrel. He identified himself as the King, Alexander, and asked Diogenes whether there was anything he could do for him.

The philosopher readily answered, "Yes, Your Majesty, would you please step aside in order not to block the sunlight."

It is a rarity these days to meet a person who is free from materialism, especially in America. One good example of an "only the tangible can be counted" attitude is the practice of tipping. To Americans, it doesn't do well to thank someone verbally or promise him that you'll return the favor in the future when someone does you a favor. You must tip the person with the tangible "greenback" (or money) right then and there.

Sometimes, you can't get a refund for merchandise you just bought if you don't present the receipt even if the storeowner remembers you. An extreme example is of a murderer who confesses the crime but the prosecutor is unable to present tangible proof that he committed the crime. He either can't be indicted, or, even if he is indicted, he can be released for not having enough tangible evidence.

On the other hand, Koreans traditionally value the non-tangible, spiritualistic aspects of human life. There is an abundance of such examples; the principle and royalty of Jung Mong-Ju who refused to yield to the founder of the Lee Dynasty that took over the country by military coup and was assassinated by the son of Lee. Also, Hwang Hee, prime minister of State, who was so poor that he had a leaky roof for a long time because he was so clean as a politician. You can attribute these differences to the fact that in the East spiritualism flourished over materialism, and in the West materialism flourished more than anything over everything.

There are many minute differences in values between the East and the West. However, I can't illustrate them all. It will suffice, however, to say that it's one of the major sources of anxiety, confusion and stress to those newly immigrated to America.

4. The Problems of Interpersonal Relationships—The Horizontal versus Vertical Societies

Koreans immersed in Confucianism may consider Americans to be barbarians. Because, unlike in Korea, the rules and regulations in America stand on the principle that "everybody is equal" and not on the "Three Fundamental Principles" and the "Five Moral Disciplines" in human relations, to which the relationship between higher/lower hierarchies, older/younger, men/women are clearly and strictly defined and adhered to.

Therefore, there are no honorific terms in English, no respect or special consideration given to the older person, and many women carry out tasks of men which no Korean woman would even think of doing. When people get to know each other a little bit closer, you go by your first name regardless of your age or job hierarchy. Many youngsters smoke and drink alcohol without hesitation in front of elders. It is acceptable to start arguing with anyone regardless of who they are if you don't like what they said or did. In one extreme case, I witnessed a teenage American son calling his father by his first name; in America, the stepchildren often call their stepparents by their first names. But in Korea, they still call them Father and Mother.

Since every human relationship in America is defined and maintained horizontally based on the ideal of "equality," this type of society is called a "Horizontal Society." To the contrary, in the social matrix of Korea, the hierarchy is clear and because everything filters down from top to bottom, it is called a "Vertical Society." If I may use an example at parties when you meet someone for the first time, Americans usually try to find out about others in comparison to themselves. How much richer the person is, if he has a better job, and how much money he makes. Whereas, the Koreans are busy trying to establish hierarchy and mutual connections in one way or another. They don't feel peaceful until the hierarchy is clearly established by finding out your age, the schools you graduated from, your graduation year, birthplace, genealogy, etc. After the establishment of such hierarchy, the relationship becomes smoother by behaving according to your position. This creates problems because Korean adults become annoyed when American youths do not pay them due respect, and the Korean youths try to obey whatever the American adults ask of them.

Once a Korean doctor who was in resident training at a hospital told me how annoyed he was when an orderly stopped him loudly in the hallway while he was mopping the floor, "Hey you! Walk on this side, not the side I just mopped up!"

He felt insulted because the man shouted at him calling "Hey!" when he could clearly tell that he was a doctor. As a result, he called Americans barbarians. However, there is no reason to feel angry, when you realize that Americans call their own president by his first name!

Of course, there are advantages to the horizontal approach to human relationships. You can express your feelings and opinions without "nunche" or looking for the other person's approval by reading the other person's facial expression, promote the ability, to act on your beliefs, and encourage the individualistic lifestyle. However, in my personal opinion, it is sometimes carried too far, creating a *laissez-faire* (or "hands off") attitude, causing many disorders at home and within the society.

Since I am a golfer, I will tell you a story I heard from my Korean golf partner. One day, he went to play golf with an American Ph.D., a psychologist, and the doctor's 16-year-old son. Whenever he couldn't hit the ball well, the young man cursed in foul language and/or threw his golf club to the ground. My partner felt very uncomfortable and annoyed by the teenager's behavior. However, what made him feel even more annoyed was the father—because he did not look annoyed by it, nor did he say a word to his son. He did not have to spank or scold him, but he could have told him what is desirable behavior in such situations! Probably, the big doctor of psychology might explain his lack of interference as showing respect to his son's freedom of expression based on constitutional rights, but I think he wasted his degree from a lack of common sense. This may explain why there is a breakdown of family and social systems in America, and chaos prevails. Being a vertical society does not mean that people in that society do not respect the rights and humanity of the lower hierarchies; but, simply that they want to establish order in the family and society. While growing up, children are still deficient in their discriminatory ability; somebody has to correct and guide them. However, it seems like people are too obsessed with equality and even the school and church do not play the guiding role. If parents do not assume the corrective and guiding role, then who else can do it? I can't help but worry about the future of America! You should not be preoccupied only with equal rights and freedom of expression. It is possible to follow etiquette while respecting the rights of others. However, due to the sickness of the society, the numbers of such parents are declining.

Also in heterosexual relationships, the idea of equal rights is creating confusion. Some take it as equality to do the same type of work. Many couples work and the wives refuse to bear children. There should be one person representing a household. If both husband and wife try to represent the household at the same time, the family will break down. Traditionally, both in the East and the West, the husband usually represents the household. Children who grow up in a family where proper order is not clearly established often develop into "problem children."

In short, there is no decorum in America that makes interpersonal relationships smooth, as there is in Korea. This is due to the difference of life-view, human-view, and social-view. These differences can generate anxiety for Koreans who are accustomed to living in a tight-knit, uniform society. At any rate, if Koreans try to interact with Americans in the way they are accustomed to in Korea, there will be friction among them. To the contrary, if they try to behave like Americans they will generate friction among their own family, friends, relatives, and other Korean immigrants. Therefore, you have to learn to maintain a balance.

5. Racial Discrimination

Race is defined as the classification of human beings according to their hereditary characteristics. This classification depends on physical differences such as skin color, type of hair, shape of face, and so on. There are so many different races on earth. They should be able to co-exist peacefully, but the problem is that they are not. Of course, there are many reasons why all human beings can't live peacefully together; namely economic, regional, racial, religion, etc. Race is only one of the reasons.

If we look at the animal world, those of the same species flock together and live together by the law of nature; the stronger prey upon the weaker. Therefore, it is a natural instinct to distrust kinds different from one's own. Human beings can't be an exception; that is, it is almost instinctual to distrust and reject different races. In other words, in general you feel more comfortable and trusting when the other person has similar facial features, similar hair, and skin color. If I may speak further, since human beings are basically or instinctually narcissistic, it follows that we like and trust others who have a similar appearance to ours, who behave and think the same way. As the founder of psychoanalysis, Sigmund Freud, pointed out that one of the two major human instincts is the maintenance of the species. It's not an easy task to completely discard such instinctual desires no matter how cultured and progressive one may be. Therefore, it is inevitable to accept others of the same race and reject those of a different race either overtly or covertly. It is called *racial discrimination* when one suppresses or invades another's basic human rights such as freedom, equality, etc. solely on the grounds of racial differences. Currently, we typically hear of whites discriminating against non-whites. However, the reason is not simply because white skin is better than colored skin. It is because white society has become the "stronger" by being progressive, aggressive, invasive, and dominant from developing modern technology early on. Of course, being the majority in number provides more power. Therefore, when non-white people immigrate to America, they become the "weaker" in two respects; first, racially and secondly in numbers.

A different side of the racial problem is that there are unwritten rules according to the expectations of the particular race and each individual is required to behave accordingly. Therefore, a Korean is expected to behave like a Korean, and Jews are expected to behave like Jews. Because of such expectations, if any individual behaves differently, he or she will be rejected by his or her own kind. For example, most usually if you marry someone out of your own race you will not be welcomed by either side and will become a racial orphan.

Earlier, I said that American society is a horizontal one based on equality for everyone. However, this is a legal ideal and not reality. Human beings do not act solely according to the intellectual function of the brain but primarily according to the forces of emotional feelings. And as mentioned before, humans already carry the rejection of being racially different others in their instinctual elements. As a result, people have a tendency to reject other people who have different skin colors and/or facial configurations. Of course, it's not limited to race; even among the same race, people reject others with different ideas or beliefs. Even if everything else is the same, if their religion is different, people throughout the world reject each other. This is an escalating problem that is threatening world peace. In the case of the United States, it is the land occupied, pioneered, and developed by whites. Therefore, whites are the majority in number; whites discriminate against non-whites. It is a well-known fact that blacks are discriminated against the most because their skin color is farthest from white. Among whites, the Anglo-Saxons possess the highest sense of superiority. It is prudent to say that the extent of discrimination is parallel to the extent of skin color away from white.

The methods of discrimination vary from overt to subtle. That is, some may say discriminating or insulting words directly to your face. Others won't rent or sell you a house or hire you for a job while making up all kinds of excuses. Some may pay you less than they pay white employees or not promote you to higher positions. Some may discriminate against you for admission to a reputable college or not accept you into a social club or country club. About 20 years ago in New York, the kids on the street called us "Chink, Chink!" This is rare now. At other times, some shouted at us "Go back to your country!" It has also become rare to hear these comments on the street. Likely reasons are because the numbers of immigrants have increased and they have become stronger; or maybe improved awareness and respect for basic human rights. An issue that makes things worse is the fact that the U.S. Congress has been trying to pass legislation to restrict some rights and social welfare benefits, which started in California in 1994, to both legal and illegal immigrants. At any rate, racial discrimination will not help immigrants adjust to American life. It unnecessarily brings on an inferiority complex, skepticism as to the benefits of immigration, and makes them feel like travelers or tenants of this country. However, these problems may be an inevitable by-product of immigration to America. Therefore, those who want to immigrate to America or who are already living in America must expect that these things can happen because, as I mentioned earlier, racial problems are delicate and complex emotional matters. They can't be overcome quickly or disappear easily. As the number of Asian immigrants grows and their united voices become stronger, these problems may gradually fade away. But, we are not at that stage—yet.

6. Inter-Ethnic Marriage

In this society, where there still is racial discrimination, inter-ethnic marriage of immigrants or their children will generate complex psychological issues. Harry H. Kitano, Ph.D., a research professor at University of California (Berkeley) and a 3rd generation Japanese-American, did some studies of Asian Americans on this issue from 1975 to 1989. According to Dr. Kitano, the longer the history of immigration of an ethnic group, the higher the number and rate of inter-ethnic marriages. The rate of inter-ethnic marriage among Japanese-Americans is 55 percent; Chinese-Americans is 45 percent; and Korean-Americans is 21 percent.

Another statistic, based on marriage licenses issued in Los Angeles County, California in 1989, reveals the rate of inter-ethnic marriages. Among immigrants it is 3.7 percent for males and 13.3 percent for females; among first generation Korean-Americans (children of immigrants) it is 33.3 percent for male, and 62.5 percent for female; among second generation Korean-Americans (children of 1st generation), 68.4 percent for male and 100 percent for female. In Hawaii, inter-ethnic marriage is much higher than in Los Angeles (79 percent versus 11 percent).

Psychologically speaking, there may be many reasons why most immigrants object to the inter-ethnic marriage of their children. However, I can mention three common reasons. First, fear of their family breaking down. They are culturally accustomed to a family-centered system and afraid that a foreigner to such a culture will destroy the harmony and balance of the family. Secondly, fear of the destruction of traditional cultural values. And thirdly, fear of being ridiculed or put to shame by friends and neighbors. In fact, occasionally you see some friends and relatives consoling such parents as if expressing condolences in a funeral home.

Some immigrants may feel that marrying a spouse from a different ethnic group adds to their adjustment in America. Ideally, and they hope, they will be welcomed and accepted by both ethnic groups. However, the reality is that they usually end up belonging to neither group. This will increase their stress because they lose the sense of belonging to either group.

But, the worst problem is yet to come. That is their child! Those children born of inter-ethnic marriage will face tremendous identity problems. They are faced with the question, "Which ethnic group do I belong to, father's or mother's?"

Ideally, they should be able to belong to either group. But, in reality, like their parents, most of them end up feeling they do not belong to either one. In reflecting this complex problem, the *New York Times* published an article on July 6, 1996, under the title, MORE THAN IDENTITY RIDES ON A NEW RACIAL CATEGORY. This article describes a family in which the father is black and the mother is white. On their child's school forms and other official papers, they sometimes check both the "white" and "black" boxes. If "Other" is available, they check it and write in "Inter-racial." When ordered to choose between "black" and "white," they resolutely leave the form blank. What frustration they have to go through!

I am sure the same trouble applies to Asians married outside of their own ethnic group; are their children "Asian," "White," "Black," or "Other"? As a result of growing pressure, the federal government has become sensitive to this issue and was considering the addition of a "multi-racial" category to the census in the year 2000. (They did not, but instructed persons to mark one or more races to indicate what this person considers himself/herself to be.) Will this help the identity problem of multi-racial children? Will this help change the feelings of people? The answer is yet to be answered.

7. Law and Ethics—"The Country of Freedom"

Occasionally, I come across people who believe that they can do anything the way they please in America because this is the country of freedom. However, this kind of thinking might facilitate finding one's self in a jail cell. It is anarchism and laissez-faire to think you can behave any way you like whether you violate other people's rights or not, and it is not genuine freedom. In genuine freedom, you are given the right to behave freely within the boundaries of law and non-violation of others' rights. In a democratic society, such as the United States, it is true that individual rights are more respected and the scope of personal freedom may be wider than in a totalitarian society, such as the freedom of public speech, publication, religion, personal assets, etc. However, when you first come to America, you will feel like there is no other place on Earth where there are so many laws governing individual behavior. You will see the struggle to prevent social chaos by instituting new, additional laws because of a fading sense of morality due to rampant materialism.

Matters that could be left to an individual's conscience and moral, ethical sense in Korea have to be controlled by law in America. It is against the law to spit or urinate on the street, smoke in an elevator, litter on the street, or even not fasten your seat belt. One recent absurd law is that the host is legally liable if his guest drinks alcohol at the host's home and gets into an automobile accident after leaving the premises. Of course, it is understandable as a desperate effort to prevent drunken driving, but what about the friendly relationship between the hosts and guests?! Anyway, this law was expanded to include taverns and bars. Now, the hosts must stop serving alcoholic drinks to their friends and guests not out of genuine concern for their friends' health, but out of fear of criminal charges.

To go one step further, you may have to force your friend to sleep over by knocking him down into the bed! What a poisonous, shortsighted rule it is that disregards spontaneous, warm, humane interpersonal relationships. When I first read this report in the *New York Times* several years ago, I became so excited I wrote a critical report that was printed in the *Korean Daily Newspaper*.

There are by-products from this type of legal policy; it creates a vicious circle in which one can do anything he/she likes as long as it's not illegal, or by deliberately finding loopholes, and coming up with more laws to contain these cynical attitudes. What makes things worse is that due to budget shortages local governments keep reducing the number of police officers who will enforce these laws. Anyway, this phenomenon seems to be inevitable since things can't be left to individual conscience or morality anymore because these have become corrupt due to expanding materialism.

Sometime ago, at a party, I met a former American GI who was once stationed in Korea. During our conversation, I asked him what was his most impressive memory and what he missed most about his life in Korea. Without any hesitation, he said it was urinating in the back street after a few drinks at night. He felt freer in Korea than in America.

You can't control all human behavior with law, and you can't watch every single human beings with so many laws. Therefore, it is not such an easy task to accept the American social atmosphere where the government keeps enacting new laws. One can perform almost any heinous behavior as long as he has a "loophole." And, a litigious attitude to sue anyone for big materialistic rewards over trivial daily matters is prevalent.

8. The Heaven and Hell of Litigation

According to an article printed in the *New York Times* a few years ago, the number of lawyers practicing in United States represents about 70 percent of the total numbers of lawyers worldwide. What an amazing fact! You may wonder how all these lawyers can make a living. As I stated earlier, there are so many laws in the United States, and naturally there will be many more criminals than you could find where there are less laws. Also, there is a prevailing attitude that you can do any deviant activity you like as long as you are not caught. So, it is understandable why there are so many lawyers practicing in America. However, you will be surprised again to hear that the large portion of their practice is to bring charges against others in civil suits for compensation. As a result, people sue each other callously for trivial matters. My impression is that everybody living in this country is suffering from litigation phobia. Since there are so many frivolous charges, you never know when, why, or how you will be sued. I do not know whether most people are aware of it, but this litigation anxiety is one of the major factors controlling human behavior in this country. Of course, there are matters that deserve ample compensation. However, there are charges brought by unethical lawyers because they need cases to make their living. No matter what the charge may be, the compensation is always monetary award. One of the reasons that there are so many negligence lawsuits is because of the *contingent fee system*. That is, the attorney's fee will be deducted from the award if he wins, but if he loses his client is not responsible for his fee. Therefore, for the client there is nothing to lose. But! The lawyer will gain more if he can win a big settlement. This is how the vicious circle is formed. Some audacious lawyers advertise through media for you to use them if you are involved in an automobile accident. Some examples of frivolous litigation are happily married couples suing each other for whatever reasons, children suing their parents over estate issues, a man suing his best friend for a minor injury after falling in the backyard of the very friend who invited him for dinner, and so on. The underlying reason for these legal actions is for large-scale compensation beyond the cost of actual damage. Of course, not everybody wins a case simply because they bring charges against the other party. But, this kind of atmosphere can contribute to the destruction of humane, trusting interpersonal relationship within the society. For this reason, America is a paradise for the clients and the lawyers who make a fortune by civil suits, and it is hell for those clients who lose.

9. Life with Insurance Coverage

Insurance is a system of protection against monetary loss. For example, in the previous section, I said that people in the United States sue each other frequently. For this reason, you must have all types of liability insurance to be able to sleep well at night. Due to America's social structure, you can't live in peace without having various types of insurance coverage. Even the government mandates that you buy insurance in order to register and own a car. So, if I should cause an accident with my car involving other people, their cars or their property, then the insurance company will pay for the damage. Since automobile accidents are the most common accidents, you must carry automobile insurance.

The next type insurance you must have is health insurance. Medical expenses are so high in the United States that if you contract a chronic, hard-to cure disease, or require major surgery, it can wipe out your lifetime savings if you don't have any health insurance coverage. There are many types of other insurance coverage such as life, disability, education, retirement, and homeowners' insurance, to name a few. There are many insurance companies offering various types of coverage.

Immigrants from countries where there are poor insurance structures tend to ignore buying coverage. Since the society of America is so complicated, you do not know when unexpected incidents will happen. Therefore, if you wish to live in this country in peace and maintain good mental health, it is essential to buy basic insurance coverage instead of trying to save money in the bank. To illustrate this point, I will tell you a real story that happened here in this country some time ago. A thief went into a house to steal some valuables. But the owner of the house spotted him and chased him out. As the thief was escaping in a hurry, one of his legs was trapped in an uncovered sewer drain. He broke his leg and was caught by the police. After fulfilling the appropriate legal punishment, he brought charges against the homeowner for payment of his medical bills and compensation for his physical damage alleging that it is the homeowner's responsibility to properly cover the sewer pipe in order to protect people from injuring themselves. I do not know the outcome of the litigation, but can you imagine anything like this in any society other than America?

10. Crime Issues

In Lao-tzu's book *Tao-Te-Ching*, he eloquently stated that if the government keeps making laws the number of crimes increases proportionally. If there was a society where there was no need for laws then it must be Utopia. Of course, it is understandable that the number of people who would violate the law will increase if there are more laws to abide by. However, since not everybody is a virtuous person, there should be laws in addition to ethical and moral codes. At any rate, the model country where this vicious circle is most strongly established is the United States. Earlier, I stated that there is no other country where there are so many laws as in America. Then, it only supports the fact that there would be more crimes in this country. The nature of crimes in America may be condensed into the product of interaction among the idiotic belief that "money is everything," deterioration of morality, and hedonism. As a result, America is the richest country in the world, but also the kingdom of crime with which no other country can compete; replete with murder, robbery, rape, drug-related crimes, etc. In the cities, people are afraid to walk around in the streets or use the subway trains after sunset. During the day, women must carry their handbags on their shoulder or strapped to their waists. At night, they are afraid to go out from fear of being raped. Some people avoid using subway trains as much as possible. Also, people spend thousands of dollars to have burglar alarms installed. Since no one knows when cars parked on city streets will be stolen and it is not possible to prevent theft with alarms and other anti-theft devices, people who own luxury cars must use paid parking garages. At any rate, the anxiety and stress coming from crimes are enormous.

I have made a trip to Korea every year for the last several years. But, I did not need to restrict my activities for fear of crime. However, due to the rapid development of capitalism, Korea is importing all the malignant social maladies from the United States and similar crimes are spreading in Korea, too. But, economic development does not always accompany social maladies. For example, Japan became one of the economic superpowers of the world, but it is known also as a country where there seldom are vicious American-style crimes. So, I feel comfortable saying that it's not "material" that corrupts a human being, but the state of the human mind. Again, I would like to repeat that a culture where ethical, moral values are highly valued leaves no room for crime to ferment.

Two main causes of intractable crimes in America are the overflow of street drugs, and illegal (as well as legal) firearms. It is a shame that the government of the most civilized country on earth is unable to contain these problems. As everyone knows, the United States is the number one country into which drugs are smuggled and consumed. There are many "drug lords" who cultivate drugs in other countries for the sole purpose of smuggling them into United States, and they have made fortunes for themselves. This fact, in turn, supports the reality that there are so many drug abusers in this country. Drugs are sold on street corners in every big city of America. From the poor to the millionaire and from the uneducated to the educated, drug abuse is taken for granted. In order to obtain money to buy drugs, the poor drug users commit various crimes, often with guns.

Currently, buying a gun in the United States is as easy as buying a Walkman stereo. This explains one reason why there are so many armed robberies and murders here. In the last few weeks, while I am writing this book, there have been five incidents in New York City alone of innocent bystanders, mostly children, who were shot to death because of gunfights between drug gangs. It is now commonplace for the police and criminals to exchange gunfights, and it is well-known fact that in many groceries and fruit vegetable stands, as well as in the residences of immigrants, there have been numerous armed robberies and murders.

The following incident occurred not too long ago in a grocery owned by a Korean immigrant in California. While struggling with a black girl who allegedly stole something, a senior female employee shot and killed the girl. This shows that it's not just the criminals who are carrying guns, but also people who want to fend off the gun-wielding criminals. What a savage world it is; a woman, especially a Korean woman, killing another woman with a gun?! Many Korean immigrants have become the prime targets of these criminals due to the notion that Koreans carry a lot of cash, keep a lot of cash at home, and that they do not report crimes to the police even if they are robbed. Of course, it's not because of a lack of laws that we can't eradicate these crimes. According to New York State law, individuals can't carry a gun without a license. But, what good is it to have a written law on a piece of paper if it can't be enforced?

There is something fundamentally wrong in dealing with crime in the United States; they handle problems *post factum* or after the fact. That is, the law enforcers try to mend the fence after the horse escapes. They lack long-range vision and just try to find ways to patch up problems for immediate results. For example, because there are so many crimes in the street, the government hires more policemen to patrol the street or enforce the punishment more strictly, and so on. I am sure everyone remembers when former President Clinton appeared on television to announce as one of his anti-crime measures, "Three strikes and you are out!" That is, if you are caught three times for committing crimes, you must serve a jail term. It was amusing to watch him making that statement on television because I felt he himself didn't believe it would work. Anyway, I have not heard that the law has helped reduce crime.

Another interesting example is that of installing metal detectors at every school in New York City when some students were found bringing guns or knives to school. What I mean is that the government attempts to stem crime by manipulating the external elements only and not the criminal mind itself. Of course, the external manipulation may help deter crime temporarily but that can't be the radical approach. The fundamental solution is a long-term plan to educate and re-educate human minds to re-establish ethics and morality in the entire society. However, no leader in this country seems to be interested in this because it is a slow, tedious, long-term process with little visible effect in the beginning.

In this chapter, I dealt with some factors that could be the source of stress or hindrance in the process of adjusting in this country. However, one should not blindly take these factors as evil simply because these are different from one's experience. There are both positive and negative sides of these, too. Once you come to live in America, you will learn to live with these seemingly stressful elements.

V

Three Types of Adaptation

Chapter IV illustrated external factors that would affect the adjustment of immigrants from Asian countries to American culture. When speaking about internal factors, the adaptation to American life is established by three elements. First are the Confucian traditions that are deeply rooted in the conscious or unconscious mind. Second is the conflict between Asian values and American values. And third is a lack of "host sense" or inferiority complex. Through the interaction of these elements, the immigrants develop one of the three types of adaptation.

1. Traditionalism

In this type of adaptation, the person unconditionally insists on keeping and following traditional ethnic values. Therefore, he invests his pride in the degree of acceptance by his traditional family, especially his parents; his indulgence in traditional ethnic values; and high education or social status. For this type of person, the conflicts are that they are reluctant to speak up against ethnic values even if those values are out of place at times and they must eventually accept the dominant American values. They are labeled as ultra-nationalists. Because they are so extreme, blind, and unrealistic or anachronistic, they can't move into the main stream of

American society. As a result they limit their lives and activities to their ethnic society.

A 21-year-old college student came to see me complaining of headaches and sleeping problems. He had been to an internist and neurologist where he had tests and examinations. However, they found no abnormalities and he was advised to see a psychiatrist. His parents were running a fruit and vegetable store from early in the morning to late at night. They were physically tired all the time from overworking. Whenever they grasped the opportunity, they would tell their son how they were physically exhausted from supporting the family, and how much expectation they had for their children, especially him, to be successful to support them when they retire.

He was a hard working and well-mannered student with good academic standing whom the teachers often complimented. His parents, however, took this for granted and at times encouraged him to do even better. He said that he felt ashamed of coming to see a psychiatrist and that he wanted it to be confidential from his parents. His problem was that his school grades recently fell and he was feeling guilty about it toward his parents because he was going against their traditional values and bringing shame to his family. He said that he lost interest in studying because he did not like to study engineering. He wanted to major in philosophy but his parents pressured him to study something more practical. He also felt anger toward his parents who were expecting him to support them as soon as he became successful. This student had been compliant with his parents' traditional values and had been behaving according to their expectations. The headaches symbolize his conflict between the traditional values of Korea and America.

2. Extremism

These are people who run to the opposite direction of traditionalism. They categorically reject and avoid anything that is Asian, including their ethnic group, with the exception of their own family members. They are the ones who try to assimilate into "perfect Americans." Their pride and self-esteem lie in how much they are accepted by white Americans. They feel Asians are not suitable to be their spouse or date and they go out with whites, the dominant ones. Actually, these behaviors reveal rejection of one's self. Therefore, they reject everything they dislike that is Asian, as well as everyone who carries the same qualities. These people become much too Americanized while they rebel against parental expectations and Asian traditions. As a result, they can't avoid feeling guilty. They can't avoid feeling conflict and anxiety because they can't hide or change their appearance. They criticize Asians for socializing exclusively with other Asians and refuse to admit that many Americans are racist. The reason for this behavior is that since they want to identify with Americans, they can't accept such an undesirable quality in them. For example, if such a person were not promoted on his job in spite of adequate qualifications, he would rationalize by blaming himself for being too humble or unassertive. At any rate, eventually they become disappointed and frustrated with themselves. Of the three types of adaptation listed here, the people who can be categorized into this group seek psychiatric treatment most frequently.

A college junior came to see me complaining of severe depression, feelings of worthlessness, and suicidal thoughts. Her father was a physician who emphasized traditional Korean values. She was urged by her parents to see a Korean-American psychiatrist for their convenience. The student was very unhappy, first of all about the fact that she came to see a Korean-American psychiatrist, and she showed a contemptuous attitude toward everything that was Korean. She had dated white boys since her high school days, but it never lasted long. Her third steady relationship with a white boy had broken up two months earlier. The break-up was motivated by her parents' threats not to pay her college tuition if she continued to date him. Although she had been vaguely aware that she couldn't deny being a Korean, it had never hit home. Then, with this incident, she became convinced that she was inevitably a Korean and started to hate herself for those ethnic roots. This led her to contemplate suicide. Of course, suicide means killing oneself. But, in this case, it was symbolic for killing what she hated which was all that is Korean. This example presents the fact that this extreme way of adjustment can also fail.

3. Eclecticism

This type of adjustment is a compromise between the two extremes described above. But, this simply does not mean to accept both extremes. Eclecticism has its own unique characteristics. There are already many model cases for the two extreme types. But, for this eclectic type, a person tries to establish a new identity by blending his own background and the new American environment. They try to preserve whatever they think is outstanding or valuable of their Asian culture while creating their own new identity, rather than categorically rejecting it. Also, they critically pick and choose among those values that are American rather than accepting them unconditionally. By believing that their current hardship is due to the political and social structure of America, they start movements to improve the image and status of Asian Americans or they participate in such activities. Some may still feel guilty for not being able to accommodate all the expectations of their Asian parents.

A twenty-two-year-old graduate student came to see me complaining of depression and feeling guilty toward his father after his death. This student had white as well as Korean friends, but had many conflicts because of his father's rigid traditional Korean values. His parents always worried that they would lose him if he married a white girl. This student subconsciously harbored a sense of shame for being a Korean descendant. However, since a few years earlier, he began to show interest in his Korean heritage and tried to propagate Korean values. Of course, his parents were happy, but he himself is still conflicted.

As the examples above illustrate, no adjustment can be perfect. Acculturation will depend upon whichever attitude you choose to take. But whichever way it is, this is a process where there always are some conflicts and some dissatisfactions.

VI

Mental Factors Leading to Mental Problems

In leading an American life, mental health problems can develop easily because of increased emotional stresses that are not experienced in one's own country. This chapter will review those mental factors giving rise to stress. Although these mental mechanisms are seen in everybody's everyday life regardless of whether it is a life after immigration or not, in the immigrant's life the degree of stress is higher. Therefore, it is possible to jeopardize one's mental health easily in the immigrants' life.

1. Stress

The word *stress* has become a part of everyday language in America. Simply put, it means psychological tension or pressure. There are many examples of stress in the immigrants' life. There are people who immigrated to America with little funds. They struggle to start a business in order to make a living. However, in spite of searching to find a business, they fail to find one suitable and must spend whatever little money they brought with them. The feelings they experience; the frustration, pressure, and tension are stress. Another example is of the high school students who emigrated to the

United States a couple of years ago, pressured by their parents' wish that they study hard and attend one of the reputable American colleges. But, because of language problems, they made slow progress toward good academic grades. The feelings of frustration, pressure, and tension were stress. Another example is of those who need to earn and save money quickly in order to bring over their family who are left behind in Korea. The feelings of frustration, pressure, anxiety, and tension from making little progress toward the goal are again stress.

At any rate, such feelings of pressure and tension that are experienced when one works hard to achieve a goal in a limited time but is unable to do so at will, can be labeled as a stress. The stress can be brought on from two sources: external and internal. The stress that a seamstress working at a sweatshop experiences when the employer pressures her to complete a certain number of dresses, and she is working hard to meet the quota, is *external.* Whereas, the stress a student experiences from pressuring himself to be the top student in the class but makes little headway is *internal.* As such, stress is a feeling we can experience easily in our everyday life, and there are many different sources of stress. Therefore, it's almost impossible to imagine a life without stress. Ordinarily, healthy people can lead their lives by managing stress well. The main source of stress for immigrants in America is ignorance about America and American life. At any rate, stress can bring on mental and/or physical problems when one experiences sudden overwhelming stress; or, when the same stress wears one down by lasting over a long period of time; or, when one experiences stress from many different sources at the same time.

First of all, stress tenses up the body muscle while accelerating the heart rate, blood circulation, and respiration. Mentally, stress can bring on tension, anxiety, or depression.

In extreme cases, stress can cause heart attacks, strokes, psychoses, and suicide. It is best to avoid stress. But, because it is nearly impossible to imagine a life without stress, it is important to make an effort to manage and alleviate stress well. Of course, the best method is to remove the source of stress, but this is not always possible. In order to alleviate stress, the most important thing to understand is how to keep your state of mind healthy. That is, for external stress, it is helpful to assume optimistically that the problem will be resolved sooner or later. For the internally determined stress, it is essential to let go of excessive desire. Of course, you have to keep making efforts to resolve the problems, too. Some other things you can do are to seek constructive recreation; go on a vacation to a nice resort, reduce your work hours, or spend some of your time on hobbies such as golf, fishing, tennis, etc. It is an absolute taboo to resort to drinking, smoking, drugs, gambling, or sexual affairs to manage stress because without fail these will add more stresses to existing ones.

2. Anxiety

An apprehensive, uncomfortable, unexplainable feeling is called *anxiety*. Like stress, anxiety is ubiquitous. From the perspective of psychoanalysis, how one deals with anxiety in childhood may lead to neurosis later in life.

There are many different factors that bring on anxiety especially in the life of immigration. First of all, the reasons one decided to immigrate might have been due to anxiety arising from life in their country of origin. After deciding to immigrate the feelings one might have had about whether or not they made the right decision, whether or not their life would be happier, the uneasy apprehensive feelings are *anxieties*. Thus, our immigration life started in anxieties and hopes, and is the extension of the same feelings.

After arriving in America, many felt anxiety from not knowing where to live, how to make a living, how to send their children to school, as well as how to avoid discrimination and falling victim to crime. As such, there is no end to what causes anxiety. It is a condition of life that follows you wherever you go, and there is no way to shake it off completely. Therefore, feeling anxiety is not intrinsically pathological, but it is rather a sign of being alive. It is a factor that arises internally, and it acts as a protective measure signaling you to prepare for what is coming soon. However, when the anxiety is overwhelming to the extent of interfering with one's daily routine, or when one handles this feeling the wrong way—it will harm their mental health. Because anxiety is an unpleasant feeling, everyone tries to remove or alleviate it. These measures, in childhood, affect the formation of one's personality, and in adulthood, may lead to the development of neuroses. If anxiety is too strong and a person is unable to control it, various physical symptoms may ensue as in the case of stress. One may experience heart palpitations, shortness of breath, hot flushes of the face, perspiration, tingling sensation of hands and feet, dizziness, trouble with sleep, loss of appetite. Along with these physical symptoms, one may develop feelings of impending doom, and as a result, may become impatient, irritable, and may create friction with others.

When anxiety interferes with one's daily routine, or is difficult to handle, it is advisable to seek professional help. If you cannot figure out why you are anxious, and the physical symptoms mentioned above persist, it is best to consult a psychiatrist. Most anxiety stems from conflicts in the unconscious mind; you will need the help of a professional psychiatrist.

3. Impatience

Feelings of impatience are again unavoidable in human life and not always pathological. The feeling you get when you hope to have something you eagerly wish to obtain is *impatience*. If you are flexible enough not to care either way, you won't have feelings of impatience. The feeling you had while waiting for the visa after you applied for immigration and disposed of your estate, the feeling you had on the airplane, hoping to reach America as safely and quickly as possible, the feeling you had waiting for transfer of the business you finally bought after arriving in America, and the feeling you had while waiting for the acceptance letter for your children after submitting an application to a fine college, are only some examples of impatient feelings.

When these impatient feelings last a long time, body muscles may tense up, the mouth may become dry, and you may be unable to sit still as in the case of anxiety. The difference between impatience and anxiety is that during anxiety the cause is not clear. But in the case of impatience, you know what you are impatient about. If this state persists or you manage it the wrong way, it may harm your physical and/or mental health. If you expect that something you want absolutely *must* happen, or are indiscriminately greedy, the impatient feelings will swell and become difficult to manage. Therefore, it is important to handle matters in a generous, optimistic, discreet, hopeful, and relaxed manner.

4. Conflict

Conflict is the emotional pain experienced in the face of indecisiveness when there are two opposing desires or conditions existing at the same time. I remember a line in a play I saw many years ago; "If I follow gold, my love will suffer; if I follow love, gold will leave me!" This is a simple example of conflict. We are all living in mental conflict. There are so many different kinds of conflicts, and it is hard to imagine a life free from any of them. However, conflicts under favorable conditions are like happy screams and do not deserve mention here. For example, a rich man may have conflicts as to which car to buy: a Cadillac, or a Mercedes-Benz. This is a conflict that should be easy to resolve without any trouble. However, if he starts suffering from insomnia, loss of appetite, and agony over this issue, he needs to see a psychiatrist right away. The problem lies in conflicts involving one's family life, livelihood, social life, and so on. It is not possible to avoid any conflict. Therefore, it is one of the conditions of life. If anyone is free from conflict, he or she must be enlightened and become a Buddha or a stiff.

We all had to experience one of the most severe conflicts of our lives before immigrating to America. Whether it was wise to go to the United States, leaving all our loved ones, our hometowns, and our mother country behind for the strange and unfamiliar land. Or, to stay in our hometown trying to stick it out where we were. The internal conflict continues even after immigrating to America and must still be going on. That is, whether to settle down in New York or Los Angeles, whether to run a business or work for someone else. If I choose to run a business, should it be a green grocery, a fish market or a gift shop? Women may ask, should I work as a waitress, hostess, or manicurist? Should I go to the church or Buddhist temple for comfort? Should I marry an Asian American or a white man or woman? In extreme cases, the question may be "should I return to my mother country or commit suicide?" The examples of conflict can go on and on. After resolving one conflict, you will inevitably be seized by another—or perhaps several at the same time.

However comforting it may be to go on resolving these inevitable conflicts one by one, when some of them can't be settled easily, mental agony may ensue. Anxiety, frustration, stress, anger, or depression may develop. At times physical symptoms such as insomnia, loss of appetite, elevated blood pressure, dizziness, chest discomfort, or heart palpitations may overlap.

Most of time, the reasons that make the conflict worse are twofold. First, picking either choice won't make the person satisfied. Second is the fact that you can't see any third solution away from the conflicting elements. For example, you don't want to own a green grocery or fish market and would rather run a fur coat shop, but you lack the funds. If the conflict continues for a long time, it will affect your mental health. These persisting conflicts may bring on neurotic symptoms or worsen an existing neurosis. However, it is not the conflicts that are harmful; conflicts are inevitable in human life. What can be detrimental is one's attitude in dealing with the conflicts.

In order to resolve one's conflicts easier and more constructively, it will be helpful to assume the following attitudes. First, remember that you can be happy either way. By assuming this attitude, you'll save a lot of time, energy, and pain in pondering which one will be better. Second, whichever one you pick, do not obsess over the negative aspects, but try to see the positive. Third, once you make a choice, stick to it. You can't be successful with anything, if you flounder.

There are a few precautions to take. That is, it is advisable to avoid completely ignoring the negative aspects or making an effort to feel blindly positive. It is like thinking that your house will be safe when the house next door is on fire. The next danger to avoid is trying to forget the existing conflicts without making any effort to resolve them. These disastrous efforts manifest themselves in the form of abusing alcohol or drugs, escaping into gambling, having sexual affairs, and so on. None of these diversions can help you resolve conflict. They may help you temporarily escape from the painful discord, but in the long run will add to your burden of carrying unresolved conflicts with the addition of alcoholism, drug addiction, financial loss, marital problems, etc. As stated before, it is a human condition to have conflicts in life. Therefore, one should make a sincere effort to face conflict and resolve it. Where there are conflicts, so there are progresses.

5. Inferiority Complex

Inferiority is defined as any type of emotional adaptation of a lower order than normally expected. In another words, the mental attitude of considering oneself as inadequate, bad, ugly, or poorer than others when he is not. Although it is an unconscious psychological state of which the person is usually unaware, nevertheless an inferiority complex affects people's speech and causes them to behave unfavorably. There are many mental complexes in the human psyche. However, there is no other detrimental complex like inferiority complex because it not only affects the individual but also the people around him.

In immigration life, there is a chance that people who have never had feelings of inferiority may develop them. Or, in those who already have them the manifestation may worsen. Many problems seen in immigrant families are the result of these feelings of inferiority. Most of all, one lacks the sense of being the host of this land because you came from another less desirable land. You feel physically different from the whites who are the host of this country, and at times you must swallow racial discrimination. Due to the language barrier and cultural differences, adaptation to this new land is slow and communication is strained. There are so many luxurious items around you but they are beyond your reach because you are still struggling just to make a living. All these may make you feel inept and inferior, which will make you irritable and unhappy. In order to alleviate these negative feelings, some may take it out on their spouse or children. Others may try to boost an injured pride by becoming the leader of an organization or trying to show themselves off in front of others. I have never heard of any other ethnic community besides the Korean-American where there are so many small organizations, churches and church elders. Of course, it may be desirable to have so many ethnic agencies and organizations to help each other, but having so many of them beyond the present need means that there are also many chief positions to satisfy the needs of the inferior minded ones. In fact, in my opinion, this trend is creating even more divisions and cliques. It is healthier to have a few major organizations to represent and elevate the position of the Korean-American community in American culture.

A person who has feelings of inferiority may manifest the following unconscious behaviors. First, he will try to pull others down to his imagined level, giving up any effort to raise himself to the level of any perceived superior person. He tries to alleviate his feelings of inferiority by disparaging others. It shows in the form of jealousy, envy, ridiculing, insulting, etc. As a result, friction with others will increase. If one spouse has strong feelings of inferiority, there will be frequent arguments between the couple. At times, this can develop into full-blown paranoia about the fidelity of the other spouse.

Second, he will exert himself too much to improve in order to reduce his feelings of inferiority. Therefore, he studies incessantly, struggles to become rich, runs around making big plans, tries to win a high government post, tries to conquer as many women as possible, etc. However, there is an interesting characteristic nature that no matter how successful he becomes, he is not satisfied or able to get over his feelings of inferiority and he must perpetuate his endeavors. If this becomes pathological, he may develop grandiose and pathological ideas such as claiming he is Napoleon, a genius, or Jesus Christ.

Third, he loses his self-confidence, gives up everything, becomes withdrawn, and never asserts his opinion. He follows other people's opinions without any critical review, and worships or obeys others who he feels are superior to him.

Besides individual feelings of inferiority, the ethnic inferiority complex can be an enormous problem. Since Koreans have a long history of invasion and subsequent rule by surrounding foreign countries, most of them have an ethnic inferiority feeling, which appears in the form of *toadyism*. A toady is a person who flatters or defers to others for the sake of personal gain or in other words a sycophant. This toadyism is a chronic illness that has been rooted in the Korean consciousness throughout the history of Korea. In the case of individual feelings of inferiority, the person tries to disparage others conversely to elevate himself. But, in the case of ethnic feelings of inferiority, people are inclined to show resignation and self-deprecation, or show unconditional imitation of the strong. In other words, he assumes the attitude that Koreans can't be helped, or he tries to unconditionally follow or crop whatever is Western. It is lamentable to see the corrupt and pathological American culture spreading widely among Koreans in Korea and America.

What is the best way to handle inferiority complex? First of all, one has to understand one's self well, and do things that can enhance one's self-esteem. Most of all, it is important not to be greedy. This does not mean not to have any desire to do things; it simply means that there is no place where feelings of inferiority can establish roots if there is no greed for material wealth or fame. If there is no greed, there won't be any emotional pain; and if there is no emotional pain, life will be more pleasurable.

6. Loneliness

It is obvious that immigrants who came ashore to this strange land where no one welcomes them will feel lonely. One may feel lonely when there is no one around, or if there is no one with whom to share warm feelings even though they are surrounded by other people. As mentioned earlier, lonely feelings are inevitable in the immigrants' life. That is, it is hard to get over the feeling of being a traveler or a tenant living in a foreign land, and feeling rejected by Americans because it is difficult to mingle with them. Also, one may feel isolated because of racial discrimination. The lonely feelings may worsen because there are no close friends and relatives as in one's native land. It will be even worse if one immigrated alone, or has not yet established a family in this country or can't find anyone to lend a hand when you need it. Koreans have a family-oriented culture where three generations often live together. Also, in Korea it is considered to be a virtue among people to exchange humane affection. For them, the loneliness will amplify when they are exposed to cold American individualism. For example, Americans do not lend big money to their friends because it is customary to borrow money from the bank to start a business. However, new immigrants usually have a hard time borrowing large sums of money from the bank because they have not yet built up credit. Therefore, some anxious new immigrants ask their friends who have been living in this country for many years to lend them money. However, since these old-timers are very much Americanized, they turn down such requests and advise their friends to go to the bank. Then they feel rejected by the friends they thought they could depend on and feel enormously lonely.

Many philosophers and literary artists like to talk about loneliness. This feeling must be handled effectively because it is one of the most influential feelings in the development of one's view of life. The works of Herman Hesse, a favorite writer of Koreans, deal with human loneliness and describe very well how painful it is. Hesse asserts that every human being is basically lonely, and this painful feeling can be alleviated temporarily by installing a makeshift bridge between individuals. Therefore, one can avoid pain and self-destructive behavior by accepting loneliness as an unavoidable human condition that will perpetuate through one's life. Some immigrants become alcoholics or drug addicts in order to allay their loneliness. Some married men who came to make money and bring their families over to America fall in love with bar girls and lose all their savings after being taken advantage of by these girls. They end up in my office because of depression.

Many Korean immigrants settle in major cities like New York. Those Korean-Americans living in rural areas away from the major cities experience loneliness even more keenly. Clearly it is important to have good communication through words and emotions in order to alleviate loneliness. I have heard that in rural areas, Korean-Americans invite other Korean-Americans or Korean exchange students to dinner for the simple reason that they are Koreans. Loneliness must be dealt with gingerly, in order to avoid harm to mental health because it often puts a person into depression or makes one lose their emotional balance.

7. Depression

When referring to depression here, I mean melancholy or sad feelings and not pathological depression as seen in Manic-Depressive Disorder. This is the feeling acquired when something does not turn out as expected and as a result one cannot see any good solution, or feels helpless. It is a common feeling that everyone experiences frequently. After saying this, I believe that there will be many times in the immigrant's life when one experiences depression. The reason is because the immigrant life is a process of re-rooting the uprooted plant from the country of origin into the unfamiliar American soil. There will be many trials and errors with disappointment in the process of making various efforts. For example, after some pondering, you may decide to run a fruit and vegetable market and open a store in a black neighborhood because there are more cash transactions than in the white areas. After struggling to obtain start-up money, however, you may suffer because the income is more meager than you expected perhaps and there may be frequent shoplifting. You might catch a shoplifter who happens to be a black woman, and if you give her a hard time, the blacks in the neighborhood may start an uproar accusing you of abusing the black woman and the black leaders may set up a demonstration against you, and boycott your store.

This is a true scenario which is one that has happened previously in New York. In spite of your appeal for justice, the mayor and his administration can't find, or are unwilling to find any solution to this racially motivated problem for many months. One can't help but feel depressed because of helplessness, disappointment and anger.

If this depressed feeling is light and temporary, one can get over it quickly. However, if it is heavy and long-lasting, it will affect your mental health and invite problems to your everyday life. If you feel depressed, all your physical functions become depressed, too. So, you may lose your appetite and develop indigestion or constipation. You may lose sleep or sleep too much; you may lose ambition to do anything and feel weak. There may be little pleasure in life and your emotions may become dull. You may avoid people, be unable to concentrate on what you do, become indecisive and feel incompetent. Also, you may feel hopeless or guilty and develop many nuisance symptoms.

Although it may be an inevitable human condition to feel briefly depressed from time to time, one must take care of it quickly and must not allow it to last a long time because it is so counterproductive. One should lead the immigrant life with a strong will not to feel disappointed no matter what happens. When you fail in one endeavor, you should pick up yourself quickly and start a different one with an optimistic attitude.

8. Identity Crisis

If you don't have a clear understanding of who you are, what you are, and where you are standing in relationship to your surroundings, you may become anxious and feel perplexed. If this state lasts a long time, you can develop anxiety and/or depressive symptoms that in turn will interfere with your mental health and daily functions. This state is called an *identity crisis*. Since this is a crisis, you must resolve this problem as soon as possible. Those who immigrate to a foreign country will experience this identity crisis sooner or later—without exception. When one becomes a permanent resident, he wonders whether he has become an American. When he becomes a United States citizen, he questions again whether he is an American or a Korean. Whenever he encounters racial discrimination, this question will become more serious. He will not know who he should identify with—either Korean or American—and will feel frustrated. He must determine which one, otherwise, he will not know how to behave in this society, will become frustrated, and will have a difficult time adjusting to American life.

I have briefly reviewed the important psychological factors that contribute to mental health problems and I have repeated many times that it is natural to have these feelings. Therefore, the problem is not feeling this way; but mishandling those feelings. When you experience one or more of these feelings, you must try to resolve them as quickly as possible.

First, think about what may be causing those feelings. If you discover the cause, the best treatment is to remove the cause. However, if you don't know the cause or see no way to resolve the problem even if you find the cause, you should consult a psychiatrist without delay.

These psychological factors may cause mental health problems. But on the other hand, these symptoms become more prominent if your emotional state is unhealthy. However, many Asians do not seem to know that they can consult with a psychiatrist when they suffer from these emotional symptoms. It often does not occur to them that these mental symptoms could be pathological and the basis for psychiatric treatment. To make things worse, many people have developed such a tolerance to these mental symptoms that they believe the disorder can be cured by will power or self-discipline. They also—wrongly—believe that it reveals their weakness if they attempt to seek help from others, and try to manage by themselves. I will deal with this issue in more detail later, but these attitudes turn easy psychiatric problems into chronic problems causing people to waste their time and money.

VII

Physical Symptoms Secondary to Emotional Problems

When one's mental state is unhealthy the person starts to manifest physical symptoms in addition to the previously mentioned mental symptoms. The physical symptoms will be illustrated in this chapter.

1. Somatization of Mental Problems

It is natural to have physical symptoms when you have physical problems. However, it may be difficult to understand if I tell you that you may develop physical symptoms *as if* you have a physical illness when in fact you don't have the illness at all and only have emotional problems. Nevertheless, it is a common occurrence called *somatization* of mental and emotional problems. This is an unconscious process and may be considered to be a symbolic phenomenon of displacing one's mental and emotional problems through one or more organs. This phenomenon has been universal throughout the ages in all ethnic groups, but it is more commonplace or without exception for Asians, especially for Koreans. Therefore, in spite of the fact that it does not necessarily mean you have physical problems simply because you present physical symptoms, people waste their time by visiting internists, neurologists, surgeons, gynecologists, ophthalmologists, herb doctors, acupuncturists, or others and bypass the very psychiatrists whom they need most. It may be interesting to think about why this somatization phenomenon is more prominent among Asians. From my personal opinion, I can present two reasons.

First, in Oriental medicine there is no concept of psychiatry. Doctors explain all diseases, including insanity, with "Ying-Yang" and the "Five Elements." That is, all organs in the body are represented by Five Elements, and disease develops when the Ying or Yang power overwhelms the organs. Therefore, Oriental medicine explains all disease in physical terms and the treatments are herbs and acupuncture, and unless one presents physical symptoms, the problem is not considered to be an illness. Also, what one thinks and feels, are all psychological and emotional matters and are not taken into consideration in making a diagnosis or treatment. This means that the person is not responsible for the illness at all.

As a result, most Koreans expect the psychiatrist to heal their psychiatric illness *alone* without their cooperative participation. However, to the contrary, in psychiatry except in the case of psychoses, each individual is considered to be responsible for the development of neuroses and personality disorders because these are caused by emotional or psychological conflicts. The second reason for so much somatization of emotional problems is ignorance and the sense of shame about psychiatric disease. Because they believe it reveals some deep weakness to complain about their emotional pains, they manifest somatic symptoms and readily complain of physical symptoms. In order to save face and not to experience shame, they unconsciously feel it's safe to express their emotional and psychological problems through physical symptoms. In light of this, it is interesting and surprising to find the statement "mind owns the body" in the medical textbook, *Dong-Eui Bo-Gam,* written by the Korean physician, Huh June, in the 19th Century.

2. Insomnia

One of the most common symptoms of somatization is *insomnia*. Insomnia manifest itself in various ways; difficulty falling asleep, frequent awakening at night, early morning awakening—to name a few. Usually insomnia that is secondary to anxiety, stress, frustration, and emotional conflict is the type in which the person is unable to fall asleep at night or to sleep deeply. Whereas with insomnia due to depression, the person is either unable to fall asleep at all or sleeps too much without feeling refreshed. If the person consistently wakes up early and is unable to return to sleep, he could have a serious depressive illness and should consult with a psychiatrist immediately.

Also, it is advisable not to resort to sleeping pills or alcohol to overcome insomnia. Sleeping pills are to be used only for a short period of time, about one month, because they lose their effect and can bring on drug addiction. Alcohol helps the person fall asleep easier but it usually prevents the person from sleeping deeply and causes frequent awakening during sleep, nightmares, and alcohol dependence. Therefore, it is strongly advised not to take insomnia lightly and consult with a psychiatrist quickly for appropriate diagnosis and treatment.

3. Headaches

There are two occasions for headaches: when there is physical pain in the head and when there are complicated, unresolved thoughts in the mind. In this section, *headache* refers to the former; that is, the physical pain caused by complex psychological conflicts or thoughts. The location of pain is either in the front, vertex, back, temple, etc. And the nature of the pain may be dull, throbbing, or sharp, and such.

The headache brought on by unresolved, complex thoughts is mostly located in the back, both temples, or behind the eyeballs. When it is acute, it clears up after a good night's sleep. However, if it is from longstanding psychological stress, anxiety, conflicts, anger, or depression, the headache won't clear up easily unless the causative factors are removed. In such case, it is very important to consult with a psychiatrist. In fact, there is no other pain as complicated as the headache, because there are about 200 causes that bring on headaches. When headaches persist constantly for a long time and wake you up in the middle of the night, it is advisable to consult with a neurologist or a psychiatrist because this type of headache may be coming from a brain tumor or vascular abnormality in the head rather than being purely psychological.

4. Gastro-Intestinal Symptoms

Koreans have a lot of gastro-intestinal problems, most likely because they like spicy foods. However, it is important to remember that psychological stresses can bring on gastro-intestinal symptoms. Usually, the first and the most common symptom is loss of appetite. Foods do not taste good and one loses the sensation of hunger. As a result, he doesn't eat as much or as often, causing him to lose weight. Therefore, in addition to emotional stress, emaciation may occur. Even if the person eats, he will have indigestion, a sense of fullness, or epigastric discomfort. This is so-called *chronic indigestion* that many Koreans experience. Repeated doctor-recommended examinations and tests won't reveal any physical problems. However, because of abdominal discomfort and epigastric tenderness, there are many who continue to use digestives, visit numerous physicians, or go from one herb doctor to another. At times, some may fall into the hands of a quack who will make a brilliant diagnosis of stomach ptosis and have the sufferer keep returning to him for treatment. This type of treatment may have a placebo effect and may alleviate the problem briefly, but the original symptoms will return sooner or later. In addition, nausea, chronic constipation, or diarrhea may result for psychological reasons.

5. Dizziness

Without any physical reasons, one may experience dizziness. In general, people believe anemia cause dizziness, but it may result from emotional pain or when one worries about their physical well-being. Of course, one may consult with physicians to determine the cause of dizziness, but it won't be helpful to go to the herb doctor and take expensive so-called tonic medications.

6. Cardio-Vascular Symptoms

When emotionally unstable, the most sensitively affected organ is the cardio-vascular system. Therefore, when anxiety lasts for an extended period of time, these symptoms will manifest themselves. One will feel heart palpitations, chest pain, shortness of breath, hot flushes on the face, etc. He then worries that he might have developed heart problems or heart attacks and may run to the emergency room. However, all examinations and tests including E.K.G. (electrocardiogram) will not reveal any cardiac problems. The blood pressure may be elevated. By this time, it becomes apparent that his cardiac symptoms are not from physical reasons, but from psychological reasons. He, then, should go to see a psychiatrist at once. Americans are well informed about these happenings, and will consult with a psychiatrist quickly. But Koreans are not well informed about these issues; they like to visit internists or herb doctors for a few years before they seek psychiatric treatment.

7. Decreased Libido

Sexual desire is the most sensitive human feeling, which disappears first when one feels nervous, frustrated or depressed and is the last to return when one recovers. When a person feels nervous, stressed out and his mind is filled with complex thoughts as in the early stages of immigration, he may feel it is a nuisance when a girl hugs him no matter how pretty and attractive she may be to him. For married couples, if one spouse develops decreased libido, their marital life may become strained and one spouse may become suspicious that the other spouse is unfaithful to him or her.

Only rarely are there men whose sexual libido becomes abnormally enhanced when anxious. This is a short-lived effort on his part to deal with his anxiety and agony by means of increased sexual excitement, which is similar to drug abuse or gambling. Decreased libido won't affect the person much when he is suffering from severe and painful mental problems. However, when it happens in the case of mild psychological problems or without any perceived psychological problems and he is unable to have sexual relations, the man becomes frightened and runs to the urologist. If there is no physical problem, which is the usual case, he should be referred to a psychiatrist. This commonly happens when he harbors discontent and anger towards his spouse. In such cases, most couples will recover through psychiatric treatment of the man or as a couple. Sometimes, a man will receive urological surgery to build a penis prosthesis (for psychological impotence) from some senseless urologist, and regret it later. He will become depressed and then seek psychiatric treatment.

8. Feeling of Weakness

This happens in a physically healthy and strong person due to psychological problems, most commonly depression. When it happens, many people, especially Koreans, start to take multiple vitamins, herbal tonic medicines, or folk remedies. There is usually a loss of appetite. But, even if he has a good appetite, eats well, and takes all those good remedies, his feeling of weakness won't go away easily because it is brought on psychologically. The feeling of weakened stamina and/or depression most commonly brings on this symptom. The individual must have psychiatric intervention to resolve the internal problems.

9. Urinary Frequency

When you feel nervous, you get the urge to urinate more often and have to go to the bathroom more frequently. However, in this case, the amount of urine you pass is little. Again, without any physical problem, one can have urinary frequency purely from anxiety.

10. A "Lump in the Throat"

There are many Koreans who complain that there is a fist-size lump in the epigastrium. This is known as one of the characteristic symptoms of Koreans in the manifestations of emotional problems, and is different from gastro-intestinal symptoms. Of course, it does not come from a big tumor mass in the stomach, but is a symbolic expression of unresolved resentment or anger clustered in one's mind. However, the person experiencing this believes that there is a mass in her throat or stomach and visits the internist, herb doctors, acupuncturists or appeals to doctors to remove the lump surgically. However, all tests and examinations of the stomach and throat come back normal. When this happens, she should consult a psychiatrist right away without further wasting her time and money.

11. Other Symptoms

There are many other physical symptoms that result from purely psychological reasons in addition to those listed above. For example, some people perspire excessively, feel cold and tingling in their hands and feet, drink a lot of water due to dry mouth, lose a lot of hair, feel itchy all over their skin, etc. These symptoms will occur naturally if the person has a physical illness. However, what I am trying to emphasize is that even without any physical illness, one can develop these symptoms purely from the mind alone, or for psychological reasons. In other words, the human mind can express its emotional suffering in many ways. These symptoms do not usually appear all at once, but one or a few at a time. When a person experiences these symptoms, he should search his mind to make connections with the emotional factors that harm mental health, such as stress, anxiety, anguish, conflict, depression, anger, etc. When the symptoms are clearly connected with the emotional factors, the possibility of the physical symptoms being caused for emotional reasons is high.

Otherwise, the problem may be either physical or psychological. Either way, it is wise to consult with an internist or family doctor first to rule out any treatable physical illness. If the results are physically normal, it is advisable to consult with a psychiatrist without wasting time and money any further even though the sufferer may not subjectively perceive any emotional problems right away.

About 99 percent of the Korean Americans that I have treated were obsessed with the idea of physical illness and visited many different medical specialists such as internists, surgeons, neurologists, ophthalmologists, ear-nose-throat doctors, or herb doctors and acupuncturists for many months or even years before coming to see me. They did this in spite of the fact that all the doctors told them there was nothing physically wrong with them.

Often, those physicians are to be blamed for not advising the patients to seek psychiatric treatment. Whenever I come across these patients, I feel perturbed by the insensitivity and ignorance of both the patients and the physicians because as soon as they start psychiatric treatment there is usually a drastic improvement. At times, there are people who need long-term treatment, but unfortunately, drop out of treatment prematurely with only minimum improvement because they have already exhausted their energy and funds in the wrong places. I strongly believe this should not happen when they are already going through hardship in adjusting to immigration life.

VIII

Psychiatric Disease and Psychiatric Problems Induced by Poor Mental Health

According to the classification of the American Psychiatric Association and the World Psychiatric Association, there are about 250 psychiatric diseases and problems. If mental status is not healthy, one can develop any of these diseases. In this book, I will comment on only those diseases and problems I have encountered and considered to be closely related to immigration life.

Mental disease can be grossly divided into two categories. The first is *psychosis;* this is what we commonly call "crazy" in layman's terms. The exact causes of this disease have not yet been determined (with the exception of those caused of certain drugs). The characteristics of psychosis are that the affected person denies reality and sometimes lives in the reality he created in his head. As a result, these people have impaired reality perception, impaired thinking, are unable to communicate with people appropriately and unable to regulate their feelings.

The second category is *neurosis.* The cause of this illness is internal psychological conflicts. The characteristics of neurosis are that the sufferer acknowledges reality and lives in reality, but distorts the reality and admits that there is something wrong with them. Of the patients I have treated, many had neurotic problems and some had psychoses.

The third category of psychiatric problems is *personality disorders* and the fourth category is *marital* or *family problems, alcohol* and *drug abuse.*

1. Psychoses

There are many different types of psychoses and of causes leading to psychoses. In this section, I will discuss only some of the most common types.

A. Schizophrenia

Of all the psychoses, this is the most common. We see people on the subway platform or in the subway train who talk or laugh to themselves oblivious to their surroundings. Most of these people suffer from schizophrenia. The characteristics of this disease are that the individual cannot communicate with other people because their thinking processes are impaired and as a result their speech is not coherent. They may have delusions, meaning that some of their unrealistic beliefs are so fixed that nobody or no reality will persuade them to correct them. Their emotions are deteriorated and as a result their expression of emotion is either dull or inappropriate to reality. They may have auditory and/or visual hallucinations. Consequently, they hear voices when there is nobody around or see things that are not really there.

There are a few different types of schizophrenia. The most common type seen among Korean Americans is the *paranoid* type. What differentiates this type from the others is that the delusions are paranoid; that is, they believe people are trying to harm them. For example, they believe that the

Mafia, FBI or CIA is trying to kill them, or they refuse to eat home cooked foods out of fear of being poisoned.

One of my female patients came to see me complaining that her Caucasian co-workers were gossiping about how inept she was as well as broadcasting her personal life and her silly behaviors through the radio and on television. Because of this delusion, she was unable to do any work or sleep, which led her to seek psychiatric treatment. In another incident, the police took a man to the hospital emergency room because he was banging the wall adjoining his neighbor's apartment complaining that he could hear the neighbors' voices talking ill of him. He bothered the neighbors complaining that they had set up video cameras around his apartment so they could watch him. A college student was taken to the hospital emergency room after he tried to hang himself with a laundry rope because he believed that his roommates were talking badly about him, and that the laundry rope was their suggestion for him to hang himself.

Koreans who are afflicted by schizophrenia are usually the quiet types. This makes the schizophrenia difficult to recognize during casual contact. However, because of delusions, a schizophrenic may become violent or commit murder or suicide. The patients are generally not aware that they have a disease. Therefore, their families must initiate arrangements for these people to receive treatment as soon as possible. However, often the trouble is that the family feels ashamed of having a relative who is a mental patient. They may try to hide this fact or feel reluctant to take the person to a psychiatrist under the pretense that he or she does not have mental disease, but a personality problem. Or even, should the patient start treatment, if his condition improves a little the family may terminate the treatment in collusion with the patient without consulting with the psychiatrist. This makes the treatment much more difficult.

Most schizophrenic patients improve through medication, but some may need to take medication indefinitely or for a lifetime. If untreated for a long time, or if they don't receive appropriate treatment or stop treatment in the middle, the symptoms relapse rapidly, make the illness more difficult to treat, and there eventually will be deterioration of personality.

B. Manic-Depressive Illness (Bipolar Disorder)

With this disease, there are prominent abnormalities in *affect* rather than *thinking*. Either, one becomes severely depressed and withdrawn or becomes euphoric and overacts as if he can conquer the whole world. These two opposing symptoms are the two sides of the same coin and they may manifest in alternation.

The characteristics of *mania* are that it gives one the grandiose delusions of being great and capable, and he will behave accordingly. He becomes garrulous, makes unrealistically grandiose plans, visits many people, actively works throughout the night without sleeping and yet without feeling tired. If anyone objects to his ideas or tries to interfere with him, he becomes angry, belligerent or at times becomes violent toward the person. For example, he believes he is Napoleon or Jesus Christ and behaves as such. In the early stages, he may sound like a very interesting person. But in the late stages, his speech will become incoherent and his judgment will become severely impaired. A woman may believe she is Cleopatra or the most beautiful woman on earth and try to seduce every man.

The characteristics of *depression* are that one feels melancholic or sad, finds no pleasure in life, and loses the desire to do anything. He avoids people; becomes impatient and irritable; feels guilty, worthless, self-critical, and hopeless for no apparent reason; entertains death or suicidal thoughts; is unable to concentrate on what he does; lacks self-confidence and becomes indecisive. Physically, he feels tired all the time, lacks energy; loses his appetite, is unable to sleep or sleeps too much; his sexual desire becomes poor. In a severe case, he may stay in bed with no energy even to lift his fingers. At times, he becomes psychotic, with delusions and hallucinations. The family must pay close attention to him because he may be a high suicidal risk.

I will illustrate an example of such delusion. There was a man who believed that he had sinned so badly that God could not forgive him. As a result, he would have brought on the destruction of the world. In order to prevent the end of the world, he would go on top of the Empire State Building and end his own life by jumping while the whole world watched him. What a grandiose delusion it is even though it is one of depression!

There are now specific drugs for treatment of manic-depressive illness. Therefore, if he receives treatment in the early stage, serious deterioration can be prevented. However, if he neglects treatment, mania and depression will alternate and eventually he will become permanently disabled. If he maintains appropriate treatment, he may be able to function normally and prevent relapse.

C. Delusional Disorder or Morbid Jealousy of the Spouse

Although this illness is classified as a psychosis because of delusions, there isn't much deterioration of affect and cognitive function as in schizophrenia or manic-depressive illness. Therefore, the afflicted person can function almost normally in the areas other than related to his delusions. The delusions are usually persecutory or jealous in nature, well structured, limited to one or two specific items, and no one can persuade the person to change his delusional thoughts.

For example, an elderly man believes that his next-door neighbor steals valuables from his apartment when he is not home. He accuses the neighbor of stealing when he misplaces his belongings and is unable to find them. He may harass his neighbors and call the police. This man is such a nice, normal person in every other respect, but when it comes to the delusion he won't budge. This is a relatively common delusion among elderly people and especially among the senile. This illness is known to be more prevalent among refugees and minorities. For the same reasons it is not uncommon among Asian Americans.

The most common delusional disorder is the *jealous type*. The typical jealous man is successful with his business, a good provider for his family and gets along well with people—but he has a malady. He suspects, without any grounds, that his wife is having affairs with one or many men and harasses her accordingly. That is, he doesn't let his wife go out alone, or make telephone calls without his knowledge. If she looks at a man or speaks to one when they are out together, he accuses her of trying to seduce the man or questions her about whether that man is her lover. If she denies his accusations, he may beat her. In some extreme cases, he may lock the apartment door from outside and take the key with him to prevent her from leaving the apartment. Or, he may put on the notorious chastity belt to prevent her from having sexual relations with other men.

You may not believe these things can happen in our modern day, but I saw such men not too long ago. The psychological mechanism of this disease lies in the unconscious fact that such a man lacks self-confidence or is unable to function as a "man." He uses this psychological mechanism as a defense against such uncomfortable feelings. Many spouses break up the marriage usually from unbearable physical and psychological abuses. (There are also female counterparts of this disease, which is seen quite often among Korean immigrants. Most Koreans are reluctant to consult with a psychiatrist, but those Korean women who are victims of physical and mental abuse by their husband's delusions, make telephone consultations frequently.) Of course, these patients never admit that they have mental problems and so almost never go to see a psychiatrist unless their wives/husbands give them an ultimatum to choose between treatment or a divorce. However, most of them do not stay in treatment or take medicine. Occasionally, I see an 80-year-old man suspecting his 75-year-old wife of having young lovers. Needless to say, these patients must consult with a psychiatrist as soon as possible. Sometimes medication helps. But don't try to talk them out of their delusions because it is impossible.

2. Neuroses

There are a wide variety of neuroses and people often joke about everybody being neurotic. There are neuroses with characteristic symptoms and there are ones without particular symptoms but that show as if they are personality characteristics. Some common types are listed here.

A. Hwa-Biung (Anger Malady)

The term *neurosis* is a western concept. As far as I know there is no terminology or concept corresponding to neurosis in the East. On the other hand, the term *Hwa-Biung* in the East, which I am going to describe, is not included in Western terminology for neurosis. In my opinion, this Hwa-Biung is the prototype of neurosis described in Korea. This term may be translated into English as *anger malady*. It has its own characteristic symptoms. Earlier, I stated that Asians somatize psychological and emotional problems into physical symptoms. They are not aware that their physical symptoms may be stemming from emotional reasons. Hwa-Biung is the only exception to this generalization because it explains that because of anger the individual has developed physical symptoms. However, most of the time, the patient cannot make the connection and complains of physical symptoms alone.

Hwa-Biung develops if you keep angry feelings inside for a prolonged period of time. The malady, caused by anger, is seen in any race or any individual, but the symptoms vary according to the race and culture. Accordingly, the symptoms of Hwa-Biung as seen in Koreans show their own characteristics. That is, she feels like there is a fist-sized lump in the epigastrium, as if she is suffocating with severe anxiety. In addition to these, she will have all the common physical symptoms of neuroses such as insomnia, loss of appetite, indigestion, general weakness, etc. However, because all these symptoms are physical, she consults with one internist after another believing that she has developed a serious physical disease. Some even ask the doctors to remove the "lump" surgically. However, repeated physical check-ups fail to reveal any physical findings to explain these symptoms. To the contrary, instead of feeling relieved she may start hopping from one doctor to another thinking the doctors made mistakes.

Hwa-Biung develops when a person could not resolve or take out her rage after experiencing unfair, infuriating feelings. The patients are usually aware of such incidents. But, because they primarily feel physical symptoms, they fail to make a connection between their emotions and their physical symptoms. They do not understand that it is a malady of emotion. The reason probably lies in the fact that in Oriental medicine, all diseases are treated based on "Ying-Yang" and the "Five Elements" theories without separating mind and body. As I mentioned earlier, when one gets emotional problems, he can develop physical symptoms by psychophysical mechanisms just as if he has a physical illness. In this anger malady, the so-called lump symbolizes the cluster of unresolved, suppressed regrets, resentment, and rage.

There are so many things in our life that can enrage us. Especially in the life of immigrants, there are plenty of matters that can make us resentful and angry. We are doing our best to adjust to a strange land, our fluency in English is poor, we must run around from early morning to late at night, and the children get into trouble because it is so hard for them also to adjust. As a result, one can be physically exhausted, feel anxious, inferior, and irritable. On top of all this, family problems can be added. I can't give the exact numbers, but I have treated many patients who were suffering from Hwa-Biung, and I am certain that many people in the Korean-American community who are suffering from this malady have not sought psychiatric help. In support of the fact that there are many patients with this ailment, Hwa-Biung was introduced in the *American Journal of Psychiatry* in 1983 by a non-Korean, a Chinese-American psychiatrist practicing in Chicago.

Without exception, almost all the patients I treated doctor-hopped from internal medicine, to surgery, to ear-nose-throat, to neurology, to herb doctors, and to acupuncturists believing that they have a physical ailment. Some who became chronically ill had visited shamans with no improvement. However, it is an emotional problem that will improve or be cured if you place yourself under the care of a psychiatrist. The longer you keep anger and resentment, the more harmful it is to one's body, mind, family and social life. So, these feelings must be resolved as quickly as possible. That is the best way to prevent Hwa-Biung and many other emotional diseases as well as maintain peace in one's mind and in one's family.

It seems that Koreans approve of drinking alcohol when they are angry. This practice is called *anger drinking* in Korean. But unless it directly helps to resolve anger, it will more likely invite additional harm or lead to taking out one's anger on other inappropriate people. Therefore, anger drinking should be avoided. The most constructive and effective way to resolve anger is, if possible, to meet with the person directly responsible for one's anger, confront him, and resolve the anger.

B. Hypochondriosis

Since I came to the United States, I have met some Americans who had lived in Korea. During mundane conversations, some of them jokingly asked me why there are so many things Koreans claim to be good for your health; remedies such as ginseng and the antlers of deer that are most popular among Koreans were useless to the Americans. I laughed with them but I realized that they picked up on an interesting side of Korean character. I do not know for sure, but this practice is probably the influence of a Taoist sage who advocated the philosophy of eternal youth. Or, by Oriental medicine that frequently and indiscriminately prescribes *tonic*.

There are so many things claimed to be good for your health. I have been to Korea at least once a year for the last several years. It seems there has been an increase in the number of so-called tonics and much more than 33 years ago when I left Korea. In addition to ginseng and deer antler, some roots and seeds, black lamb, snake soup, and such are being touted. Now, the number must be over a few hundred so-called remedies. Of course, this supports the fact that Koreans pay a lot of attention to their health and they worry about it.

Simply put, hypochondriosis is a neurotic disease in which one believes he has contracted a serious physical illness (with no actual physical illness present) or believes that he has become physically weak. It is understandable that under severe emotional stress, one may worry that he had contracted a major disease with only trivial somatic sensations. However, normally, they don't become obsessed with the idea and feel relieved when the physical examination or test results are normal. However, those people who are afflicted with hypochondriosis firmly believe that they have developed a serious disease in one of their organs, or have become physically weak. Further, they lose their temper with people who try to persuade them to the contrary, demand more tests, or treatment for the disease they believe they have. Also, they usually do not trust the conscientious physicians who tell them there is nothing physically wrong and they go doctor-hopping. For example, if one happens to cough, he starts to worry that he may have contracted tuberculosis or lung cancer. If he gets a headache, he starts to worry that he may have a brain tumor. If he gets mild abdominal pain, he thinks he has stomach cancer. If he experiences a mild burning sensation when urinating, he believes he has severe venereal disease. Examples such as these can go on and on. At times, the location of the organ changes from one day to another, such as its the heart today, stomach the next day, and the brain on the third day. Some who complain of tiredness and weak feelings consume tons of vitamins or herbal tonics for long periods of time with no improvement. This may be from depression. For the people watching them, it is irritating, stifling and pitiful. But for the patients, it is a serious reality.

Hypochondriosis is closely connected to anxiety or depression and is a chronic illness. Therefore, it is strongly advised that the patient be brought to the psychiatrist as soon as possible for consultation and treatment even though it may be a difficult task to persuade him to see a psychiatrist.

C. Anxiety Neurosis

One feels anxious for no apparent reason, is unable to concentrate on anything, the pulse becomes rapid, hands and feet become cold and clammy, he passes urine frequently, is unable to fall asleep easily, becomes sensitive to everything, etc. These are some of the symptoms of anxiety neurosis. When symptoms become worse, one may have panic attacks; develop palpitations, shortness of breath, perspiration, chest pain and feels he is faced with impending doom. This attack lasts from a few minutes to several hours, experienced from a few times a day to a few times a week. Sometimes, it happens no matter where you are, or at other times it is in crowded or open places.

When they start to have panic attacks, people frequently run to the hospital emergency room from the belief that they are having a heart attack. However, all the tests and examinations rule out a heart attack. Also, a complete physical checkup does not reveal any physical problem either. Since these are physical and psychological manifestations of uncontrollable anxiety, you must seek psychiatric treatment.

D. Depression (or Depressive Neurosis)

Depressive symptoms here are similar to those of the depressive phase in manic-depressive psychosis mentioned earlier, but the degree of depression is lighter and does not present any psychotic symptoms such as hallucinations and/or delusions. It belongs to neurosis. It is the most common problem of all the problems seen in psychiatric practice. Different from Korean-Americans, Americans do not hesitate to seek psychiatric treatment whenever they feel depressed for various reasons.

I have been in psychiatric practice for over 30 years, but I have yet to see one Korean-American who came straight to see me for the reason of mild depression. If that is the case, then does that mean depression is only for Americans and not for Koreans? Of course, that is absolutely not the case. Since human feelings are similar in both the East and West, Koreans can develop depression as commonly as Americans. Then, one may ask, why don't Korean Americans seek psychiatric treatment for depression?

If you have read this book from the beginning, you may already have the answer. Most Koreans consult with a physician complaining of physical symptoms that accompany depression. For that reason, they go to see an internist or neurologist, with the complaints of insomnia, indigestion, headache, palpitations, loss of appetite, fatigue, etc. They go through all kinds of special tests and procedures depending on their physical complaints. Of course, they will be told that all the tests and examinations are normal. If their medical doctors are sensible people, they will advise the patient to see a psychiatrist or will refer the patient to one. Otherwise, they will try to treat these patients solely with medication that usually is futile. Some patients may go doctor-shopping looking for a physician who can find some physical problems.

93

(They probably feel that if you are going to have problems then physical ones are better than emotional ones.) They may also go to Oriental herbal doctors, get some expensive herbs and take them for extended periods of time hoping that will cure their depression. One interesting thing is that both Koreans and Americans suffer from physical and mental symptoms when they are despressed. But Americans usually complain of mental symptoms and consult with a psychiatrist from the beginning whereas, Koreans focus on the physical symptoms and consult with *physical* doctors first.

There are many different reasons why one becomes depressed. In general, one gets depressed when things in life don't go your way and you feel trapped. Therefore, it is understandable that there will be a lot of depressed people in the immigrant life, because you can't adjust to American life, because you can't make a living quickly, because of friction between husband and wife, because your children create problems, because your pride is hurt, because of lasting inferiority complex, etc. The list is endless. As such, the reasons stem from psychological pain and an individual's personality make-up. Therefore, it's absolutely essential to have treatment by a psychiatrist. Besides, many excellent antidepressants have been introduced lately. So, it is most effective to have combined treatment of psychotherapy and medication preferably by the same doctor.

E. Obsessive-Compulsive Disorder

There are people who cannot shake an unwanted recurrent thought or thoughts and must perform seemingly meaningless ritualistic behaviors in order to fend off the recurrent thought. The former is called *obsession* and the latter is called *compulsion.* There are many different types of obsessive-compulsive manifestations. The most common illustrations are the "checking" type. For example, this is when a person is not sure whether he locked the door or turned off the gas stove, starts to feel anxious, keeps going back to double-check over and over, causing him to lose sleep the entire night.

Another common example is the "cleaning" type, in which he is obsessed over contamination with germs or dirt, and has to wash his hands or take a shower many times a day while disregarding his other responsibilities. In some cases, he uses up a few bars of soap in a few days and causes his skin to peel. A nasty example is a man who is obsessed with the belief that he emits a foul odor from his body and constantly sprays his body with deodorant. He goes from one doctor to another in search of the source of the odor, and sometimes goes through unnecessary surgery of the axillary sweat glands. Another troublesome example is a woman who becomes obsessed with the thought of stabbing someone whenever she sees a sharp object like a knife and becomes anxious and restless. So, she constantly avoids or hides the sharp objects. If these people are stopped from carrying out their compulsive behaviors, they become so anxious that they may develop panic attacks. Because it is a disease of anxiety that is difficult to manage and interferes with one's life directly, one should consult with a psychiatrist as early as possible. There are now specific medications to treat this condition.

F. Phobia

There are many things people are ordinarily afraid of, such as darkness, heights, wild animals, snakes, etc. However, fear of these things in average people is short-lived, acceptable, and does not interfere with routine daily functioning. But, there are people who are afraid of absurd things or situations such as going out of the house, going into a crowded place, riding elevators, crossing bridges, etc. Some others are afraid to make presentations in front of a group, avoid going to social gatherings, or are fearful of benign pets. I am sure many people have a fear of flying. The problems with these people who have phobias are that they have to avoid these fearful situations and objects, which in turn will restrict their life. In severe cases, he cannot leave his house unless accompanied by a person who he feels he can trust. If these phobic patients are exposed to the situations or objects they are afraid of, they will go into the state of panic attack. Phobia is one of the relatively common neurosis that again requires psychiatric treatment.

G. Post-Traumatic Stress Disorder

After experiencing a life-threatening traumatic event, some people may develop lasting mental and/or physical symptoms long after such event is cleared. Some examples of such events are natural disasters, exposure to combat situations during war, being robbed at gunpoint, being raped, serious automobile accidents, etc. The traumas referred to here are mental and not physical traumas. It is natural for anyone to develop various mental or physical symptoms such as insomnia, loss of appetite, anxiety, depression, nightmares, avoidance of similar situations, etc. In most people, these symptoms subside in a few to several weeks. However, there are people who continue to suffer from these symptoms beyond the reasonably acceptable period of time.

The unusual problem with this neurosis is materialistic compensation for the trauma, or secondary gains. In the

United States, people, without exception, hire a lawyer and sue the other party who they believe caused such trauma, or sue the government for compensation. Because of the expected monetary compensation, these patients consciously or unconsciously won't give up their symptoms until the lawsuit is resolved. These patients must understand that of course they deserve to have compensation but they should not become greedy and should utilize their better judgment that their self-esteem is more important than money.

H. Character Neurosis

In this type, there are no clear-cut and specific symptoms as described in the above types. The person suffering from character neurosis shows one of the three behavior patterns in life that are excessively pedantic, impulsive, impatient, aggressive, meticulous and self-centered, or much too compliant and pleasing, or annoyingly indifferent to everything in life, and so on. This neurosis is built into their character. To some extent, many people show similar qualities from time to time but in this neurosis, the difference is that it is lasting, quantitatively excessive, inflexible, and often they feel unhappy with their self. Because the neurosis appears to be a personality trait, many take it for granted and think there is nothing anyone can do about it. But, they are dead wrong. Character neurosis is a neurotic condition that can be treated with psychotherapy, and the best treatment is psychoanalysis. With some exaggeration, I will say that all Koreans are neurotic—meaning that everyone has character neurosis especially the first type. I have seen many people who are unhappy with their lives or with themselves because of character neurosis. Some sensible ones may start treatment, but due to their impatience, or rather because of their very character neurosis, they unfortunately drop out of treatment prematurely.

There are some more different types of neuroses in addition to those mentioned above. However, since this book is not a psychiatric textbook for professionals, I am going to omit the less common ones.

3. Alcoholism

It is rare to see people as fearless of alcohol as Koreans. Medically speaking, alcohol is not a nutritious, non-toxic substance. It is not a medicine, nor is it a stimulant. It is a poisonous substance.

Alcohol inhibits the function of all human organs and destroys all the cells of the body. Due to the body's increased tolerance to alcohol, and to the mild euphoria it produces in human beings, people can become addicted to alcohol. In spite of all these negative contributions alcohol makes, many people think drinking alcohol is a fanciful thing to do, consuming large quantities as a manly gesture, and they will boast about their drinking. Also, some people believe alcohol will lull your worries.

This is a far-fetched misunderstanding, created by the society and the culture. According to legend, the famous poet, Lee, Tae-Baik of China lived his life splendidly. So did the wandering poet, Kim, Sock-Kot. What a fascinating story it is that they were able to recite beautiful poems instantly after a drink! However, don't be fooled by the notion that glasses of wine inspired them to create such beautiful poems. It is easily understandable by the fact that not all drunkards are beautiful poets. However, unfortunately there are many people who are brain-washed by these fascinating misunderstandings, and drink when they feel happy, when they feel unhappy, when they bump into an old friend, for their business's sake, in order to relax after a long day's work, in order to sleep better, for this reason, for that reason—and so on. The list is endless and I have yet to see one who is unable to drink from lack of excuses.

There are many different kinds of alcoholic beverages, but they can be divided into three large categories: namely beer, wine, and hard liquor. Many believe alcoholics drink hard liquor only, but that is not the case. They may prefer hard liquor in the beginning, but often end up drinking wine or beer due to physical weakness. Some take beer as roasted barley tea and insist that it is good to quench thirst and helps their digestion. However, it is an unfounded allegation, because the content of alcohol in a mug of beer, a glass of wine or a shot of whiskey is more or less the same. I have never seen anyone drinking beer in a small whiskey glass or wine glass. Therefore, it does not help anyone to determine whether a person is an alcoholic or not, by what kind of alcoholic beverage he drinks.

One goes through a few different stages before reaching alcoholism. The first stage is abuse of alcohol. The second stage is psychological addiction. The third stage is physical dependence and the final stage is death. The first stage of alcohol abuse is characterized by gradual increase of alcohol consumption and often drinking alone using all kinds of excuses in addition to socially acceptable situations like a party, business gathering, family dinner, etc. Especially alarming is when a housewife starts to drink alone during the day or hides liquor in the house and avoids people by drinking in the closet. Regardless what the excuses may be, if someone starts to drink alone or starts to have "blackout spells," it is a bad sign.

The second stage of psychological dependence is characterized by a strong craving for alcohol, a feeling of restlessness, and an inability to concentrate on his work unless he quenches his thirst for alcohol.

The third stage of physical dependence is characterized by his inability to abstain from drinking because his body starts to act up. About 6 hours after his last drink, his hands begin to shake and his body feels restless and nervous. If he gulps down a drink hastily, all the shakes and anxiety clear up like magic, and his sense of well-being will be restored. (This is the reason why many alcoholics must have an "eye-opener" in the morning.) However, if he doesn't supply the needed alcohol to his body in time, he will go into a *withdrawal syndrome* that may be life-threatening. The body will shiver, perspire profusely, and consciousness will become cloudy. An alcoholic may start to hear voices or to see things, and may lapse into epilepsy-like seizures. This is a medical emergency that must be treated in the emergency room of a hospital. Visual hallucinations of insects or animals are common. The drinker may see a cute puppy, a pink elephant, or a lion. Of course, these are phantoms but they are so vivid to him that he may actually stroke the puppy, or in trying to escape from the wild animal he may fall off a high-rise building and die.

By the time one becomes physically addicted, all the organs of the body start to show signs of malfunction. Starting with the most familiar disease, cirrhosis of the liver, the stomach, pancreas, heart, bone marrow, and brain are badly affected, hastening the road to death. It is a well known fact that cirrhosis of the liver is common among alcoholics. Koreans are notoriously well known to the world for being infected with viral hepatitis, and as a result there is much cirrhosis of the liver and cancer of the liver. In addition, drinking alcohol will facilitate the development of liver cirrhosis and/or liver cancer.

In the larger cities of the United States, liver cirrhosis used to be the fourth highest cause of death. In those chronic alcoholics whose brain cells continued to be destroyed by alcohol—in addition to physical and natural death of these cells—they may develop symptoms such as *senile dementia* at a young age. Their hearts become weakened and many alcoholics die from heart attacks. In addition, some die from acute pancreatitis.

It is almost laughable that these chronic alcoholics who are dying from physical complications assert that they don't drink much and that they have full control over their drinking. For these reasons, treatment becomes delayed, or they never receive treatment. Therefore, when you evaluate alcohol problems, it's useless to ask the drinker how much, how often, or what kind of alcohol he drinks. What you need to know is what effect their drinking has on their overall quality of life. That is, whether there are family problems due to frequent arguments between the drinker and his/her spouse. Does he have problems on his job due to frequent absenteeism, late coming, poor functioning due to intoxication, or being warned by his superior, or being fired from his job due to his drinking? Whether he was arrested for DWI (driving while intoxicated) or for disorderly conduct. Whether he caused an automobile accident due to intoxication, etc. If the answers to some of these questions are *yes,* he may be already an alcoholic or alcohol abuser. If, however, he develops the aforementioned withdrawal symptoms when he suddenly stops drinking, he is without any question an alcoholic.

Of course the life of the immigrant is dull and tiring. However, if we call America the paradise of drunkards, the Korean community in this paradise is a haven for drunkards as good as the marriage of paradise and Nirvana. There are tasty appetizers and alcoholic beverages at every restaurant. There are standing bars, piano bars, karaoke bars, and night-clubs here and there. There is popular Korean music soothing the homesick heart and there are pretty, attractive Korean girls at hand to wait on you. You don't need to envy the king! The taste of wine may be out of this world! However, as the popular singer, Na, Hoon-A sings in his song, "The Far Away Home," what a painful feeling the drinking heart may be carrying! More frustrating is the fact that no matter how much you drink, it will not wash away the pains and sorrows. If anything, drinking will make these feelings worse as you are staggering down the road toward alcohol addiction.

Alcoholism is a *disease*. It is wrong to think strong will power can easily fix it because the problem is not weak will power. As any disease, if you start treatment in the early stage, it will be easier to cure the problem. Usually, the reason why one begins to abuse alcohol is due to emotional conflict. Therefore, it is important to resolve such conflicts with the help of the psychiatrist before alcohol starts to engulf the person.

If you notice the following two signs, they are the early symptoms heading towards alcoholism; the first one is called *tolerance*. That is, the amount of alcohol you need to feel high gradually increases. The second is called *black-out spells*. That is, you cannot recall what happened the night before while you were drinking. If any one or both of these signs occur, it is strongly advisable to consult with a professional doctor.

It is a big misunderstanding to believe drinking alcohol will help to resolve your problems. Rather, you will end up adding one more difficult problem to the existing problems. Therefore, you should not make any rash decisions to use alcohol.

I touched on it briefly before, but the side effect of drinking is not limited to physical complications. There are numerous examples of family problems or broken families due to drinking; losing friends because of violent, destructive behavior under the influence of alcohol and being unable to carry on a decent social life. A person can't function adequately on the job because of frequent absenteeism, lateness, or an inability to concentrate on his work. He may be reprimanded or warned by his supervisor about his performance, or he may be fired from his job. Those who operate machines may experience accidents resulting in injuries to self or others. Especially those who drive their cars under the influence of alcohol may get into accidents killing innocent other people or injuring himself.

When you drink, it may increase your self-confidence to drive a car. But to the contrary, your judgment and ability to operate the motor vehicle becomes impaired and you can easily cause fatal accidents. Therefore, the United States government emphasizes through public education just how detrimental alcohol is, and those who drive while intoxicated are arrested and punished severely even if they don't cause accidents.

According to the *Korea News,* as a result of strict handling of drunken driving in California, the number of DWI (driving while intoxicated) incidents has declined. Surprisingly, however, now most of the DWI arrests are of Korean Americans! This is a good example of the extent of Korean ignorance about the effects of drinking alcohol and the poor judgment they have in regard to drinking alcohol.

It is strongly advised that those who are concerned about their drinking should consult with a physician who specializes in treating alcohol abuse problems before it is too late, instead of bluffing about their ability to control their drinking.

As a mental health provider for Korean-Americans, I am concerned about alcohol abuse because judging from my psychiatric practice experience there are so many people with this problem. What I am especially concerned about is the fact that there are so many people who drink excessively while taking it lightly; that there are many people who do not seek treatment in spite of having withdrawal symptoms, and that even if they do start treatment they do not continue long enough.

4. Drug Addiction

Since the North American continent is the number one consumption market of illegal drugs in the world, it is clear that immigrants who are living in such a society also are affected by it. Especially, when you become exhausted from living the American life, you may get the urge to escape from such a hard life and lay hands on the drugs that are easily available in the street. "I'll just try it once!" becomes twice, and then three times—and eventually you become irretrievably involved.

There are many different causes for drug abuse, and there are many different kinds of drugs being abused. Of course, one can say that the person abuses drugs essentially because there are defects in his character. However, the direct causes can be divided into three categories. The first is social reasons. It is seen most commonly among teenagers but also often seen among mature adults. They share drugs at parties like drinking alcohol. Although it is called social, sometimes one may abuse drugs by the pressure or urging of his friends.

The second is from misusing prescribed habit-forming drugs. That is, misusing, prescribed drugs different from doctor's orders for a long period of time. No matter how pitiful a patient's appeal is the doctors must pay attention to this in order to prevent such a thing from happening.

Third, those who chronically abuse drugs sold on the street. Often they have underlying depression and many of them have character disorders. Some of them use drugs as self-medication for underlying schizophrenia or depression and anxiety.

The abused drugs may be divided into five categories.

A. Narcotics

There are many different kinds ranging from naturally cultivated to synthetics. The most commonly abused are heroin and morphine, then, codeine that is used to suppress coughs and Darvon, a painkiller. One out of ten heroin addicts dies each year, and the most common cause of death is accidental overdose. Also, because a user commonly takes injections, often with dirty needles, he may easily contract hepatitis, pericarditis, pneumonia, vasculitis, and worst of all there is a high chance of contracting AIDS (auto-immune deficiency syndrome).

B. Sedatives and Hypnotics (Tranquilizers and Sleeping Pills)

Although you need a doctor's prescription to buy these drugs, you can easily buy them in the street. Since all of these drugs are addictive, you must use them according to the doctor's directions and only when these are indicated as a treatment. Most commonly heard names are Valium, Xanax, Dalmane, Ativan, and barbiturates. If one abuses these drugs, the symptoms are similar to alcohol intoxication. If anyone who is addicted to one of these drugs stops taking them abruptly, he will go into withdrawal symptoms as is the case of alcoholism. In severe cases, he may develop epileptic seizures, coma, or death. Therefore, people who abuse these drugs and/or alcohol must receive treatment under a doctor's supervision.

C. Stimulants

Drugs belonging to this category are creating major problems in the United States. In Korea, *Speed*, known in Korea as *Hiropong*, is most popularly abused. According to one of the daily newspapers, the *Korea News*, an underground manufacturing factory of *Speed* was discovered by police in Los Angeles some time ago. Further investigation revealed that they were connected with the underground manufacturing organization in Korea. Drug abuse may be because the world is filled with serious and depressing matters, but in the United States stimulants are the most commonly abused drugs and have become one of the major social issues.

The most commonly abused stimulants are amphetamines, dextroamphetamin, methamphetamine, cocaine, and crack. These drugs may be swallowed, or in case of cocaine may be sniffed or smoked. Crack is a highly addictive form of cocaine that is smoked. The reason that crack has become such a problem is that it is much cheaper than cocaine, easy to make, and a person can become completely hooked after using it just once.

Amphetamines have been abused for a long time as weight reducing diet pills as well as stimulants. The symptoms shown after taking these stimulants are euphoria and then nervousness, agitation, talkativeness, violence, etc. The physical symptoms are heart palpitations, temporary elevation of blood pressure, loss of appetite, and insomnia. At times, in chronic use, symptoms that mimic schizophrenia (split mind) may develop. If these stimulants are stopped abruptly, withdrawal symptoms such as severe fatigue, anxiety, fear, depression, twitching of the whole body may develop. Specialized physicians must provide treatment for amphetamine abuses.

D. Hallucinogens

There are people who cannot look at reality as it is because it is too painful and they prefer to distort it. Hallucinogens do this for them. When one takes hallucinogens by mouth, by sniffing, or by injection, his senses become twisted causing objects or his own body to appear distorted, auditory or visual hallucinations, euphoria, or at times the illusion that he has become highly enlightened. Physically, he will experience heart palpitations, perspiration, blurring of vision, and widening of pupils. Some of the common hallucinogens are marijuana, mescaline, LSD, and PCP (Angel Dust). There usually are no withdrawal symptoms when one stops using them, but in chronic abuse, delusional psychosis may develop.

E. Inhalants

These are the volatile substances easily available in every household, such as gasoline, glue, solvent, paint, aerosols, cleaning fluids, nail polish remover, etc. Mostly, children inhale fumes or vapors from these substances. The effects are mild euphoria, mental confusion, and staggering. In severe cases, one may develop toxic psychosis, convulsions, or coma. In worst cases, these fumes may destroy kidneys, liver, heart or bone marrow and lead to death. Since children and teenagers abuse these substances most commonly, parental education is urged.

We have made an overview of drug abuse. It is a worldwide social burden, and everybody is struggling with this problem. The harmful effects of drug abuse are enormous. Human dignity and moral ethical values are destroyed. Robbery, gang wars, and murder are rampant. The silent worldwide killer, AIDS, is rapidly spreading without people's awareness. In the Asian-American community, drug abuse has been surfacing increasingly. One should take caution not to fall into momentary temptation and destroy one's self and family.

5. Habitual Gambling

In the immigrant community, one of the major problems emerging is *habitual gambling*. People afflicted with this problem believe that money is the source of all their difficulties and money is also the only answer to resolve all their problems.

Gambling flourishes where there is plenty of stress. Then, it is self-evident that gambling will be a problem in the immigrant community where there are a lot of people troubled by enormous stress from trying to adjust to American life and making a living in this new world. As reported by the Korean-language daily newspaper, this alarming problem is a serious matter.

What, then, is habitual gambling? We all play with friends and relatives where betting is involved on holidays.

These types of social activities are accepted in any culture as recreational activities. In these games, the amount of betting is limited to acceptable, reasonable amounts not to burden the participants. Therefore, there is no pride connected with these activities; regardless of whether one wins or loses, there are other life matters more important than gambling, and there is no emotional pain following whether one gambles or not. To the contrary, however, the following characteristics are of habitual gambling.

1. There are strong obessions that he wants to gamble and secure money to gamble.
2. He gambles with larger amounts of money than he initially intended and for longer hours, more frequently.
3. For the sake of excitement and thrill, he keeps raising the betting amount and bets more often.
4. If he does not gamble, he becomes anxious and irritable, and unable to do anything else.
5. He keeps gambling in spite of losing money with the excuse that he wants to be even.
6. He gambles when he should be doing house chores or working on the job.
7. He gambles sacrificing the social, occupational or family matters, and sound recreational hobbies.
8. He gambles in spite of mounting debts.

Of course, habitual gamblers know what they are doing is wrong and repeatedly say they are trying to remedy their problems. But, they cannot easily give up their obsessions because they cannot let go of the climactic pleasure and excitement gambling brings them. Therefore, in psychiatry, habitual gambling is labeled as one of the diseases of poor impulse control. They borrow money in order to continue gambling, and habitually lie or engage in unlawful activities because of mounting debts. As a result, they invite troubles with their family, social, and occupational life.

Some examples of habitual gambling are mind-boggling. There are people who lose their houses by gambling one night at a casino. Others go bankrupt from gambling while playing golf. At times, habitual gambling is brought on by other psychiatric illnesses. Therefore, those suffering from habitual gambling must first consult with a psychiatrist to rule out any causal psychiatric disease and receive psychotherapy and medications.

6. The Problems of Children

This issue is such a complicated and important one that it needs a big separate book. Of course problems of children are not limited to the immigrant community or Asian-American families. This is a serious problem in American society as well. But, because of the special circumstances of immigration, problems of children in the Asian-American community present a complicated picture from various causes.

First, let us divide children into two categories; 1.5-generation, and the second generation. Second generation children are those who are born in the U.S.A. from immigrant parents and 1.5-generation children are those who were born in Asia and immigrated to United States as children. Although these two categories of children share many common problems from being raised by Asian-born immigrant parents, each category of children presents unique characteristic problems. Before I go any further, I would like to say that I am not ready to touch on third generation issues because there isn't much reporting or research on them.

According to my experience and observation, second generation children, present more of the problems seen in non-immigrant American families than 1.5-generation children who present more of the problems stemming from immigration life. Regardless of background, the pictures shown externally are similar.

A. The Appearance of Children's Problems

What are children's problems? I will list some examples; there is a sudden drop of academic grades, they lose interest in studying, go to game rooms instead of going to school, frequently fight with other kids, are left back in the class or worse expelled from school. If parents are asked to see the school principal or guidance counselor who are concerned over the child's behavior or academic grades, the parents must accept it as a big warning sign and take immediate action to correct them. Worse examples are running away from home, sexual acting out, drug abuse, stealing, robbery, joining gangs and gang fights, carrying weapons, suicide attempts, or as an extreme example, murder.

B. Causes of Children's Problems

It is hard to blame only one factor as the cause, but we must consider many factors working together in complicated ways. However, the most important and crucial causal factor is a troubled or dysfunctional family. In another words, we cannot blame the child alone or their mixing with a bad crowd. If any child's academic marks drop or his unacceptable behavior problems continue or he commits a serious crime, do not blame your child alone but consider whether there are serious and lasting family problems.

There are a variety of family problems we should all consider that bring on anxiety, fear, and mental stress in children. For example, threats to a secure home such as financial problems causing worry about basic support or one of the parents suffering from a chronic debilitating illness can be very upsetting for a child. One common problem in immigrant families is both parents going to work from early morning to late in the evening. This results in a lack of protection and supervision of their children after school. Parents must remember that this causes severe anxiety, fear, resentment, and mental stress even to teenage children. Of course, it is understandable that they immigrated to America for a better life and are anxious to establish a financially stable life by earning money quickly. But they have to weigh which is more important, raising their children well and healthy or sacrificing child rearing in order to earn money quickly. Sensible parents can easily judge which has priority.

Many parents misunderstand that to be good to their children is to make them materially affluent. They rationalize their blind efforts to earn money as being the best way toward this purpose. But, it is more important for the parents, especially the mother, to stay with the children spending time together, caring for them, protecting them, and giving them affection in order to prevent their children from feeling anxiety, fear, and stress. Many parents claim that they came to America for the sake of their children's education. If that is truly the case, they have to live up to their claim by making their best efforts to raise their children emotionally healthy.

Some parents come to America and leave their young children behind in order to concentrate on working to quickly establish financial stability. Their relatives or the grandparents raise the children for several years until the parents are ready to bring them over. Even worse, there are parents who send their young children back to their old country because both mother and father have to work. There, their relatives or grandparents raise them for a few to several years until they are more financially comfortable. In both examples, although their own parents do not raise the children, their surrogate parents care for them. They may not have the anxiety and stress of staying at home without parental supervision and protection, but they most likely will develop resentment and anger from feeling that their parents abandoned them and/or don't love them. As a result, even after rejoining their parents later, they are unhappy, depressed, abuse drugs, and show various behavior problems.

In November of 1985 in Los Angeles, six Korean-American high school girls ran away together from their parents' homes. Eventually, they were found and rescued from drugs and prostitution. They all gave the reasons for their behavior as disappointment, resentment, and rebellion against their parents working until late hours in the evening. Also, in 1988 in New York City, one of the Korean-American youth gang members who was arrested for possession of illegal weapons blurted out, "I don't have parents!" to the reporter who offered to call his parents for him. If he thought he was an orphan it is nothing but a factual statement even though his parents were well at home. When his father received the call from the reporter, he lamented, "When I am doing hard work over 12 hours a day for my son and living with the hope that he will become successful, I can't understand why he becomes so twisted as this!" His mother also sighed, "His parents work hard to feed him well, clothe him well, send him to school like any other well-to-do kids, and I can't figure out why he behaves this way!"

As shown in these examples, it is not in the best interest of the children for the parents to provide material comfort and luxury items for young people by working hard and earning money only to leave the children alone and unattended. These types of parents tend to overspend and give big allowances to their children thinking they are being generous to their offspring. But, this is nothing but a bribe to wash away their guilty feelings for not being really caring parents. To the contrary, this attitude will only make things worse for the children by encouraging their vanity and unacceptable behaviors. Then, what is more important to give children than material possessions? I already said it: warm parental affection, gentle care, appreciative communication.

In the late 1940s, an American psychologist, Harry Harlow, reported a study he conducted using monkeys. He made two different mother monkey dolls, one with milk feeding nipples while the entire body was wound by wires. The other was clad with velvet clothes but without feeding nipples. The baby monkeys liked the latter one that they could make close body contact with and feel cozy. He also reported that adult monkeys raised without a mother are not social and not able to mix well with other monkeys. They usually have problems with their sexual life and mothering of their own babies. This research can be applied to humans and supports the argument that for children it is far more important to be hugged by parents with affection and love than to be fed well.

C. Parental Conflicts and Children's Behavior Problems

The most significant of all family problems that causes children's behavior problems is long-standing conflict between their mother and father. Since this is an important issue, I will handle it separately. All aforementioned family problems are seen mostly in immigrant families. But, conflicts between parents can be seen in immigrant families and their first- or second-generation family as well as any family aside from immigration. Earlier, I stated that behavior problems should be considered differently between the first generation immigrant (meaning second generation children) and the 1.5-generation immigrant. But, that is based on the cause of their behavior problems and not on the manifestations of behavior problems. The reason being that causes may be varied and different but manifestations are more or less the same. The immigrant parents of first-immigrant generation children are generally financially established and stable. Therefore, they have more time to spend with their children and room to care for them. Consequently, there are few behavior problems with their children stemming from these causes.

The common causes of these first-immigrant generation (meaning second generation) children is the anxiety, fear, and stress due to long-standing parental conflicts and disputes. When parents don't get along, they don't have emotional room to take good care of their children and the children become hungry for parental affection. At times in these families, one can see deviation of loving care; one parent indulges one child, the other parent indulges another child. This complicates the existing parental conflict and aggravates the family problems.

Now, let's consider how a long-standing parental conflict can produce troubled children. Firstly, children are very sensitive. Although they may pretend they are not aware of anything, they actually are very conscious of conflicts between their parents. They shiver from the fear and anxiety of their parents breaking up the family, getting divorced, and abandoning them. However, young children cannot express these fears and anxiety verbally and directly. Instead, they express their feelings through unacceptable, destructive behaviors, such as running away from home; participating in crime, drug abuse, and indiscriminate sexual behaviors; cutting school; and in, extreme cases, attempting or committing suicide. These abnormal behaviors stem from two psychological mechanisms, one of which is a direct reaction to their anxiety and fear. The other is an unconscious mechanism, in which the children try to divert parental attention from their fight to who are behaving badly as mentioned above. This is in a sense, an effort of martyrdom.

Secondly, on the part of the parents, when parents became tired of fighting each other they turn on a child. In order to have a temporary cease-fire, they unconsciously pick one of their children, make him into the "bad child" and start to gang up on the child together. If a child has already started to act badly, most likely he or she will be the one they pick. By this mechanism, the mother and father may briefly develop the illusion that they are a congenial and agreeable couple. However, it is clear that their underlying conflicts will continue unresolved. This child is called the *scapegoat*. It may be one who was already acting badly through martyr-like behavior in order to save their home. Or if not, he cannot help but act badly due to parental abuse and become a troubled child. Most of the troubled teenagers I treat are from this type of dysfunctional family.

D. Difficulties of Immigrant Life and Children's Behavior Problems

We reviewed family problems causing troubled children. Now, I would like to focus on the problems occurring outside the house and how they are related to unacceptable behavior of children.

Children also experience the conflicts and difficulties stemming from racial discrimination, language difficulty, cultural differences, and differences of value systems between

East and West. In my opinion however, their suffering is greater than the parents' in the beginning of their immigration. The reasons are that the grown-ups make contact with people limited to their business, but children are forced to make contact with other children, teachers, and other people in the widespread context of education. They may also be subject to ridicule by other children because they are still immature. They will perceive more sensitively any trivial matters because they are going through emotionally unstable and sensitive developmental stages.

The most common reason that Asian-American immigrant children join school gangs and get involved in gang fights lies in the fact that they are trying to handle the anguish and resentment brought on by the mistreatment they receive at school. The following example illustrates my point. A white student called a 10th grade Korean-born student who immigrated to America with his parents a year ago a "chink, yellow monkey!" The student became angry and a fight broke out. The white student got the help of a few friends and the Korean-born student was badly beaten. A school guidance counselor came to the rescue, broke up the fight, and asked them the reason for their brawl. The Korean-born student explained to the teacher, in broken English, what had taken place. But, the teacher believed what the white students had told him. They clearly had lied when they said that the Korean-born student spat at the white boy. The Korean student was reprimanded, warned not to repeat the same behavior and ordered to have his parents come to school to see the school principal. He became so frustrated and helplessly infuriated because his poor English was not good enough to convince the teacher otherwise. He went home and told the story to his parents with strong emotions and tears of frustration, hoping they would go to school, clear the false accusation and avenge the unfair treatment he received. However, because both parents work and were not comfortable with their English they declined to go to the school to see the principal. In order to merely smooth out the problems instead of directly tackling them, the parents tried to persuade their son to apologize to the school authorities and tell them he wouldn't repeat the same behavior. Trying to overcome this major disappointment, he went to a Korean gang, who beat up the white kids who had attacked him. As a result, he got the protection of the gang, but he had to pay the price. The gang started to use him in their crimes. He was forced to participate in robbing a Korean store and was quickly arrested. This example illustrates that the way children deal with problems that occur outside of their home is very much influenced by how well their parents understand and approach the problems. Therefore, it is essential for parents to show an active and positive attitude in dealing with their children's problems and show them they care for them and are protective of them. In this case, the parents could have opened their store later in the day and they could have asked someone who speaks English fluently to go to the school with them so as to set the record straight for their child. One cannot overemphasize the importance for children to grow up with the belief that they are not alone and their parents are there for them whenever they need protection, support and caring.

E. The Relationship Between Immigrant Generation and Immigrant First-Generation Children

Although both generations of children are descendants of immigrant Korean parents, their values are often widely different. The first-generation (meaning second generation) children carry mostly American values and ways of thinking, whereas the immigrant generation children have traditional Korean values and ways of thinking which in turn create communication problems between these two groups. Immigrant children are fluent in Korean and talk to each other in Korean but are poor in English. Whereas first-generation children, on the other hand, are poor in Korean and use English most of the time. Therefore, these two groups cannot get together well. Even in the same school, immigrant children socialize among themselves and the first-generation children socialize among themselves or with white children. I had an opportunity to provide group therapy for immigrant children who had been in the United States less than two years at a high school. It was apparent that their feelings toward first-generation children were that of dissatisfaction or hostility. They blurted out that they don't speak Korean although they are in fact Korean, they are arrogant and belittle the immigrant children, they don't show homage to them as "older brother," they avoid them, etc. On the other hand, the first-generation children who were born in this country criticized the other group for trying to impose their Korean values and ways of thinking on them. The girls are especially critical of immigrant male students' behavior as out of touch with reality and foolish.

A short while ago, an older immigrant student stabbed a younger first-generation student to death at a high school. The immigrant students interpreted this shocking incident as the surfacing of the struggle between immigrant and first-generation children or between Korean values and American values.

It is amazing to learn that there is such a delicate relationship established between these two groups in spite of the fact that they both have immigrant parents. However, according to my observation, in time as the immigrant generation children become fluent in English and accustomed to the

American way of thinking the tension between the two groups becomes more relaxed and they become friendly. But, I have not seen an example of first-generation children learning to speak Korean fluently and mingling with immigrant children well.

In summary, I have reviewed children's behavior problems or immigrant-generation teenagers' problems. The main causes of children's behavior problems lie in a dysfunctional family life. Dysfunctional families result from longstanding parental disputes, excessive parental absence, a lack of parental affection and care, and too little constructive communication between the parents and children. Therefore, it is strongly advised that when the teenage child begins showing mild behavior problems or extreme behaviors like attempted suicide that the parents consult with a psychiatrist who can provide family therapy without delay.

F. Couples' Problems

Another problem stemming from having poor mental health is incessant discord between a couple. According to American statistics, half of married couples end up in divorce. Statistics for Korean-Americans are not to that extent but the number of divorces is steadily increasing. According to one statistic, about one third of couples in their 30's break up their marriage.

Marital problems that I've treated seemingly indicate a direct correlation to the stress of American life. While they were still living in Korea, they got along very well. But, they started to accumulate enormous stress from the combination of running a business and making a living in this strange land. They did not have time and emotional room to exchange warm affections due to long hours of exhausting work. Some kept failing with their business endeavors, and the husband began drinking out of frustration and took it out on his family; that perpetuated their marital problems. Some other couples went out to work on different jobs because of financial difficulties, and one of the couple started to have an affair with another man or woman on the job. Some developed pathological jealousy that he or she didn't' have while living in Korea. In the family where the wife went out to work, the man felt that his wife's assertiveness and power were elevated whereas his authority had declined.

The real causes of marital problems do not actually lie in aforementioned external or superficial factors. Paradoxically speaking, if husband and wife love each other dearly and their relationship is satisfactory, then they can get over stresses from immigrant life easily through mutual help and support. In other words, it is difficult to conclude that stresses of American life alone are the most important and direct cause of marital conflicts.

The beginning of friction in a marriage is in communication problems. This is different from having a communication problem due to poor English in the beginning of their American life. They don't have problems in hearing what the other is saying since they both use same native language. The problem is not grasping the meanings or understanding of what the other is trying to convey.

Then, what are causes of communication problems? Those come from the personality differences and differences of viewpoint, value systems due to different family or individual cultural differences. For example, between an obsessive-compulsive husband who is an organized, meticulous, perfectionist and a hysterical wife who is vain, social, glamorous, disorganized, and attention-seeking, it is clear that they will have problems with what the other wants or is trying to communicate. Also, if the wife is raised in a family devoted to Christianity, where Confucian-style ancestral rituals are ignored, and the husband was raised where traditional Confucian and Shaman rituals are observed, it is not difficult to understand that there will be communication problems. Therefore, in order to avoid any friction due to communication problems, it is important to clarify what the other person wants without assuming on your own.

There is another factor that perpetuates a couple's discord. That is, one or both insist that only he or she is right, and expects the other to change what he/she wants or tries to change the other person. However, a couple is a system, in which if one makes a move the other also makes a move in response. Therefore, it is not possible to expect only a one-sided change without making a change yourself. So, a couple must live together dynamically by forming a harmony with mutual change and accommodation.

The third factor to consider is that one or both have either a strong inferiority or superiority complex. In this case, one or the other easily twists or misunderstands the other person, or looks down upon and belittles the other, inviting frictions. Even if you don't have these complexes, if the couple treats each other with mutual respect there can be peace and happiness.

As I mentioned earlier, martial discord is the most crucial factor in creating a "problem child." For the sake of sound mental health and development of a healthy personality, it is of utmost importance to have a loving, harmonious relationship between parents. But, it is important not to perpetuate frictions or blame the other without resolving the problem. It is advisable to seek professional help if frictions cannot be resolved quickly. Since marriage is the process of adjusting to each other by filling up the gap between two different characters and building harmony between them, one should try the best not to break up the relationship without making the best efforts. Therefore, unless one spouse has a mental illness such as pathological jealousy, one should not lightly entertain the thought of divorce. It is advisable to consult with a psychiatrist who can provide marital therapy. Both should be involved in this type of treatment. There are two people involved in marriage, both of them are equally to blame when there is a lasting marital conflict. Don't try to change the person, try to change the thoughts.

G. Personality Disorders

There are many different types of personality disorders; some common ones are antisocial, borderline, dependent, histrionic, narcissistic, obsessive-compulsive, paranoid personality disorders.

A personality disorder is a life-long, ill-adaptive pattern of thinking and behavior about which the person doesn't feel anything wrong. Of course there are many genetic factors, but the development of personality also has a lot to do with environmental factors. If a child grows up in a mentally unhealthy environment, his personality formation will be influenced. The personality disorder that is most greatly influenced by environmental factors is the *neurotic personality,* or as some call it *character neurosis.*

This is most clearly described by one of the great, neo-Freudian psychoanalysts, Karen Horney. According to Horney, everybody is born with "Real-self," which is the core force for development of oneself into the most constructive and happy person. But, if in early childhood, the environment is unfavorable to such growth, the child develops *basic anxiety.* In order to deal with this anxiety, the child develops many neurotic elements that are built into her personality. As a result, the child's personality will become either self-effacing, expansive or resigned. When these children grow up, their personality will be expressed respectively, as people who cannot say "no" to others, try to be the winner in everything they do, or don't care about anything in their lives. These neurotic personalities are different from genetically determined characteristics and are susceptible to change through psychoanalytic treatment.

Many Korean-Americans present these neurotic personalities rather than neurotic symptoms like phobias, anxieties, obsessive-compulsive behaviors. Normal personality and neurotic personality should be differentiated clearly.

IX
Psychiatric Treatment

There is a unique characteristic in psychiatry different from other specialties in medicine. Other categories are divided into internal medicine in which diagnosis is made and drugs (if necessary) are prescribed, and surgery in which diagnosis is made and operation is performed. However, in the practice of psychiatry, psychotherapy is the most important treatment modality in addition to making a diagnosis and prescribing drugs. As a result, there is no other specialty so difficult to master and render treatment. Because psychotherapy is a talking therapy and the effects are not immediately apparent, there is an erroneous belief that anybody who can talk can provide psychotherapy. However, just imagine how difficult it would be if you have to use same tool named "talking" everyone else can use! For that reason, some people compare the psychiatrists' tongue to the surgeon's scalpel. That is psychiatrists' "talking" is the knife used to operate on the "mind." Therefore, if untrained or unqualified people use their tongue in the name of providing psychotherapy they may cut up another's mind and cause more injury.

Of course, I do not mean to say all psychiatric illnesses are without exception treated with psychotherapy. There are other treatments and there are different types of psychotherapy as well. I would like to review them briefly now.

1. Psychotherapy

Psychotherapy is defined as the treatment method using verbal means targeted for people who have emotional problems for the purpose of symptom alleviation or removal, correction of deviated behaviors or habit, and constructive development and growth of maladaptive personalities. Therefore, psychotherapy should be strictly differentiated from unprofessional so-called *counseling*, which utilizes personal advice, education consultation, persuasion, command, spiritual inspiration, and so on.

Psychotherapy can be further classified by different criteria such as whether the subject is an individual or group, long-term or short-term. But the most scholastic criterion is whether the therapist can help the patient to understand what caused the illness and help him overcome it, or to treat the patient without emphasizing the cause of the illness.

There is an important fact all psychiatric patients must remember. That is, when you go to other doctors such as an internist or surgeon, all you have to do is say what is bothering you or what symptoms you have. Then the doctor will examine you, give tests, make a diagnosis, prescribe medicine and/or give you orders on what to do and what not to do. However in psychiatry, telling the psychiatrist what bothers you is not sufficient because the psychiatrist cannot do everything for you alone. You must cooperate with the psychiatrist and work with him according to his direct and indirect guidance. That is, you cannot just sit and wait for him to prescribe drugs, give you advice and instructions. You must verbally express what you feel and think without screening or holding back.

Psychotherapy can be divided into the following categories. First, helping the patient understand the cause of his disease, development of symptoms and help him get over the problems. This type of psychotherapy is *insight psychotherapy*. Second, when the patient is unable to deal with reality because of anxiety, fear, or stress, rather than digging into his mind, protecting and supporting his mental strength. This treatment is suitable for those patients who have no mental strength to withstand digging in their mind—as with some neurotic patients or most psychotic patients. This type of psychotherapy is called *supportive psychotherapy*.

In short, psychotherapy aims to alleviate emotional pain and symptoms, thereby restoring daily function by helping the patient understand his conscious conflicts, re-arranging his mental capacity so he can deal with his mental problems and utilizing his mental capacity to its fullest extent. Unlike in psychoanalysis in psychotherapy you don't deal with your unconscious mind or early childhood memories and do not aim for personality change. Therefore, the treatment lasts a much shorter duration.

Psychotherapy is suitable for rapid treatment of some patients suffering from neurotic symptoms such as depression, anxiety, phobia, obsessive-compulsive disorders, and patients who are suffering from severe stress, anxiety, or depression due to acute life difficulties. All psychiatrists are well trained to provide the type of psychotherapy, but for Koreans and Asians, the most difficult treatment to offer is this psychotherapy of verbal means. I already mentioned earlier that the reasons this is difficult are manifold. Coming from a cultural background where it is considered to be a merit *not* to be verbal and *not* to express one's inner feelings or thoughts easily; the influence of traditional Chinese medicine in which mental problems are not dealt with at all, resulting in somatization of mental or emotional problems, and an impatient temperament. Therefore, most Korean and Asian patients expect the doctor to give them drugs or injections, instructions on what to do, and fix them at once. As a result, most of them feel it is a waste of time and money to converse with the psychiatrist other than telling him the symptoms, what bothers him, and how much he is suffering.

However, psychotherapy is the main stem of psychiatric treatment and it usually takes a longer time than in other medical specialties. To participate in psychotherapy, patients must cooperate with the psychiatrist by revealing their inner feelings and thoughts, and the process usually requires weekly visits for a minimum of a few months. But, most of these patients come only a few times at most. This makes the psychiatrists frustrated because their hands are tied to provide the most effective treatment. Koreans and Asians must become educated and acquainted with psychotherapy so as to alleviate their emotional sufferings more quickly.

2. Psychoanalysis

This is the most in-depth verbal therapy in which human unconsciousness is addressed in addition to symptom alleviation. Psychoanalysis aims for understanding the unconscious psychological mechanisms of one's self and becoming a happy person by changing one's personality into a more desirable one so as to be contented with oneself. In other words, psychoanalysis is the essence and acme of verbal therapy. It is the most suitable treatment for those intelligent people suffering from neurosis who are discontented with their personalities, existentially unhappy with their lives, and for those who are ambitious to live their lives more meaningfully by changing their personalities.

It would be ideal if everybody could go through psychoanalysis. But there are limitations, because psychoanalysis is for those who have strong willpower and motivation. The drawback is that it takes a long time to complete and therefore financial affordability should be taken into consideration. Besides, psychoanalytic training for the doctors takes several years of extensive and expensive training. Therefore, there aren't many certified and truly qualified psychoanalysts available. However, it is a highly recommended treatment to those who can afford it.

3. Group Therapy

This is a form of psychotherapy provided to a group of several patients at the same time, instead of one-to-one. In most cases, about ten patients are adequate to form a group. People may think group therapy is a cheap treatment for poor patients because it is in a group setting. However, that is an absolute misunderstanding. Group therapy has its own place in psychiatric treatment. Group psychotherapy is excellent to treat neuroses. Trying to provide psychotherapy for a group of patients is not group psychotherapy, nor it is an individual psychotherapy in a group setting. In order to become a group psychotherapist, one needs to have specific education, training and experiences. Here I limited my discussion to specific group psychotherapy modalities, but there are many different kinds of groups that provide supportive group therapy, such as groups for schizophrenia, Alcoholics Anonymous, etc.

4. Marital Therapy

This is a therapy to save marriage when there are long-standing marital problems that the couple is not able to resolve between themselves. As emphasized before, children can only grow emotionally healthy if their family is healthy. Also, the couples themselves will have trouble with their social and occupational lives due to stress from their marital problems. Therefore, it is advisable to seek professional marital therapy in order to avoid the complications of marital conflict.

At times, it helps to consult a priest, minister, monk, or counselor. But if that does not help it is desirable to have marital therapy before making up your mind to end the marriage. The characteristics of this therapy are that the subject of treatment is the relationship between husband and wife, rather than with individuals. But, since it is imperative to grasp the individuals' backgrounds, personality, difference of personality, and cause of friction, it is more difficult to provide marital therapy than individual treatment. Therefore, it is important to find a therapist who is well trained and qualified in marital therapy.

5. Family Therapy

In this therapy, all family members become the subject of treatment. As in marital therapy, each individual is not the subject of treatment but the focus is on the relationship among the family members. The goal is to help the family to live in harmony together. In general, a family consists of parents and children, but if there are other important family members living in the home such as grandparents, aunts, or uncles then they should be included in this therapy too.

As mentioned earlier, this treatment is essential when children create behavior problems, when frictions between parents and children continue, and when frictions between parents persist. This therapy is a difficult but an excellent treatment that can be only provided by a well-trained and qualified family therapist.

6. Hypnotherapy or Medical Hypnosis

Hypnosis itself is not a treatment. Anybody can learn how to hypnotize a person. Many entertainers and magicians use hypnosis. Shamanic ecstasy is also a hypnotic phenomenon. When you are totally absorbed in a play or movie, or the euphoria when two lovers caress each other, are also hypnotic trance states. If psychiatric treatment is provided when a person is in this hypnotic state, the effects could be dramatic. When a psychiatrist is trained to induce hypnosis and use it in a psychiatric treatment, it is called *hypnotherapy* or *medical hypnosis*. Here, the therapist provides psychotherapy or behavior therapy after inducing the individual into a trance state. Hypnosis is not magic, nor is it a myth, nor is it putting the person into sleep. So, the term hypnosis is a misnomer because *hypno-* means sleep. Every human being has the ability to go into a trance. Therefore, hypnotherapy has the advantage of being useful for uncooperative patients as well as for short-term therapy. The application is widespread from smoking cessation and the treatment of neuroses, hysterical symptoms, psychosomatic symptoms, chronic pain, etc. This treatment is usually safe and harmless. Medical hypnosis is getting popular and there are many prospective patients who request hypnotherapy.

I will illustrate the most dramatic example that I have treated with hypnosis. An eighteen-year-old girl became paralyzed in all four limbs and suddenly blind after an argument with her mother. She was forced to stay in bed, immobilized. Her mother became frantic and called me urgently because I had started treatment with her a few weeks prior. Since I was well-trained in medical hypnosis, I was not as excited as she. Otherwise, I should have advised her to take her daughter to the emergency room. I made a house call, which I rarely do, where I put her in hypnotic trance, explored her feelings, gave her post-hypnotic suggestions and left. A few hours later, I got a call from her mother again who was now excited in a different way and reported to me that her daughter had fully recovered. It was really a dramatic treatment episode. If I had been a psychiatrist who didn't know anything about hypnosis, I am sure the patient would have gone through all kinds of tests after hospitalization.

7. Counseling

This word has become a popular word lately, but this should be strictly differentiated from more involved psychotherapy. Counseling is the most simple and superficial treatment in which patients are supported and re-educated to adjust to their life better. Mainly, the counselor tries to help the patients change their environments, gives some practical advice, or tries to help them use more of their own strength. For example, a counselor will advise you to take a vacation, change your job, or may advise a couple with marital problems to go out to dinner once a week or go away on a vacation together. It is used by less trained counselors for temporary management of crises.

8. Zen Meditation

When I say Zen medication here, I don't mean any religious ritual. Like other oriental religions, Buddhism contains five elements: psychology, ethics, philosophy, religion, and the extraordinary. Of these, I am going to deal with the subject of human psychology.

There is no such concept as *psychotherapy* in the Orient as in the West, but there are a lot of similarities between Zen meditation and Western psychotherapy. "Everything in this universe is created by the mind;" this principal theory of Buddhism is comparable to the belief that "Every human behavior is determined by mind," the principal theory of psychoanalysis.

Zen is cultivating methods aiming at becoming enlightened about one's own true nature and becoming a Buddha. Therefore, it should be practiced under Zen masters in a structured way, whereas in psychoanalysis, one tries to understand the self by expressing what he feels or thinks to the analyst. In Zen meditation, one illuminates one's mind in silence. These two seem contrasting, but what is aimed at is very similar. We as Asians must be proud of the development of such a great psychotherapeutic methods in the Orient.

These days, many Westerners are practicing Zen meditation and studying Buddhism. It is not difficult to assume that there are many mind-healing elements in Zen Buddhism based on the fact that there are so many Western psychoanalysts, psychologists, and Christian theologians who indulge in the study of it. However, Zen meditation is not very helpful for psychoses such as schizophrenia. It is greatly helpful for people who are suffering from neuroses and human miseries.

9. Behavior Therapy

In this therapy, the main focus is on abnormal behavior, disregarding patients' feelings or thoughts while using methods and result of experimental animal psychology. For example, if a person has fear of speaking in public then the therapist will slowly expose him to similar public settings until he gets used to it and overcomes the problem. Another example is a person who has a fear of riding in elevators. Again, the therapist takes the person into the elevator, in life or in imagination, little by little until he can ride it alone without any fear. As illustrated in these examples, the therapist will not deal with patients' childhood or feelings other than fear. Therefore, it is like taming animals. There are a few different techniques besides the one I used as an example, that is a gradual exposure to the fearful situations.

Behavior therapy is applied when the patient is not interested in psychotherapy at all but has, for example, phobia or obsessive-compulsive disorder. Sometimes, it brings on excellent results.

10. Pharmacotherapy (Medication)

Drugs used in psychiatry are divided into 3 categories; those used for psychoses, anxiety, and depression. There are more than several dozens of them, and many are indicated for specific diseases. The use of these drugs is very complicated and none of them can be used effectively unless prescribed by a psychiatrist. Most psychiatric diseases require medication. For psychoses, drugs are the only and best treatment. For other diseases, drugs may be used until troublesome symptoms subside, and the patient then continues with intensive psychotherapy.

The tranquilizers and sleeping pills (hypnotics) commonly used for anxiety are strongly habit-forming or addictive, and must not be used for periods of time. It should be remembered that most psychiatric problems handled in psychiatry can't be treated by medication alone except for psychoses, but instead are treated in conjunction with other treatment modalities.

What I learned through my treatment of Asian-Americans, especially Korean-Americans, is that many patients are reluctant to take drugs and refuse to take them. They often start medication but at the first sign of side effects, they discontinue the drug without consulting with the psychiatrist and will not resume any medication. Some patients take drugs for a few weeks and stop them on their own accord, thinking it's harmful to take drugs for a long time even if they are urged to continue them. In cases of psychoses or depression, these patients will quickly relapse, which makes further treatment even more difficult. On the other hand, there are other groups of patients who demand medication alone when they need to have psychotherapy as well.

Another thing the readers must remember about psychiatric drugs is that they all have side effects; that once a suitable drug or drugs are found, patients may have to continue the same drug for many months, years, or a lifetime. Therefore, these drugs must be used under the supervision of a psychiatrist.

11. Electro-Convulsive Treatment

This used to be called *electric shock therapy* and turned off any favorable feeling toward it. This is one of the oldest treatments that were popularly used before revolutionary drugs were introduced. It is still used for patients who do not respond to any medication, especially those who have severe depression or psychoses. Often the result is excellent. Although it sounds cruel because patients receive electric shock, there has been great progress in the usage of this treatment. Therefore, you can hardly see anything cruel about it, and it has become very safe.

12. Treatment of Alcoholism and Drug Addiction

Alcohol and drug addiction has been socially and traditionally condemned and avoided by people for many decades. As a result, their treatment has been neglected by medicine. However, these addiction problems have become one of the most serious social problems worldwide. Due to the fact that physicians avoided dealing with these problems, there is a shortage of doctors to treat these patients—leaving non-medical, under-qualified people with little training to fill the void. As a result, treatment centers for alcohol and drug addiction have "mushroomed" all over America. But, for many years, the quality of treatment has shown little improvement, and gives the impression that many centers are merely business endeavors. Some so-called "rehabilitation centers" are like involuntary hotels where patients are confined for a month or two, prevented from drinking, and are discharged back to society in a sober condition. However, many of them resume drinking as soon as they leave the centers. It is a serious problem. In my opinion, alcohol and drug addiction must be treated by specially trained psychiatrists because addictive diseases affect both the mind and body at the same time. Detoxification from alcohol or drugs alone is not sufficient. Intensive follow-up treatment must be provided to maintain sobriety and prevent relapse.

In the case of alcohol addiction, there are drugs that may curb cravings for alcohol, and drugs that will induce extremely unpleasant physical symptoms when patients drink alcohol while taking this medication. However, the results of these medications are not very impressive.

One of the historical self-help groups called Alcoholics Anonymous, or "A.A." is in itself not a treatment but an excellent adjunct to medical treatments. These groups are numerous and widespread all over the world but unfortunately are not popular in Asian countries. Historically, the problem in treating alcohol and/or drug addiction has been the notion that addictions are the result of weak willpower. But, nowadays, this notion has given way to the concept that addiction is a disease. Since the research and understanding of this disease is making good progress and because it is a big social problem, treatment has become very active. However, physicians and psychiatrists are still not school-educated and trained to deal with this problem more effectively. The treatment approach for alcohol and drug addiction differs from the treatment of psychiatric patients. Therefore, the general public must seek specialized physicians or psychiatrists for this treatment.

13. Treatment of Children

The treatment of children requires a child psychiatrist. In order to become a child psychiatrist, one to two years of additional training is required. Children over twelve years old are handled either by a child psychiatrist, adult psychiatrist, or an adolescent psychiatrist. The evaluation and treatment of children is difficult because they don't cooperate as well as adults, and communication is difficult. Therefore, parents and family members are often included in children's treatment, and often family therapy is indicated.

In summarizing psychiatric treatment, most therapy is carried out by a combination of two or three treatments, and most commonly, medication and a form of psychotherapy.

X

The Use of Facilities in Psychiatric Treatment

It is important to know what type of treatment providers and facilities are available for appropriate treatment.

1. Psychiatry is Not a Specialty That Deals Solely with "Insane" People

This idea is the by-product of the 18th century when there was no clear understanding of mental illness and mental patients were confined in dungeons and often shackled without any treatment. Nowadays, there is a better understanding of mental and psychological problems. The medical specialty to treat these problems is psychiatry. Therefore, this specialty deals with so-called insanity or psychoses, all emotional pains, couples' problem, children's problems, family problems, substance abuse, etc. As a result, mental patients are proportionally much less common than patients with anxiety, depression, adjustment problems, neuroses, etc. As mentioned earlier, psychiatry is not just for pathology, but also to help someone become a better and happier person. Nowadays, people don't feel ashamed of going to a psychiatrist, nor do they try to hide it; rather, many people who are in psychoanalysis brag about it or are proud of it.

It is better to have any disease treated in the early stages. Psychiatric problems are not an exception. It is important not to make problems chronic and difficult to treat. As I stated earlier, instead of consulting with a psychiatrist to begin with, many Asian-Americans visit internists, neurologists, and other medical specialists, herb doctors, acupuncturists, and so on because they become preoccupied with the physical symptoms even if they are told there is nothing wrong with them physically. After wasting so much time and money, they eventually end up with a psychiatrist. The public and non-psychiatrist specialists must be educated about this problem and refer patients to psychiatrists without wasting time.

2. Psychiatric Emergency

Emergencies in psychiatry are referred to situations where immediate threats to life exist such as suicidal/homicidal risk or when uncontrollable destructive, violent behavior occurs. Also, a state in which the person loses his judgmental ability and the ability to protect himself due to acute psychosis. In such emergency, if the person already is seeing a psychiatrist, the patient or his family must contact the psychiatrist immediately and follow his instructions. However, if the patient does not have a psychiatrist yet, or is unable to contact the treating psychiatrist, the patient or his family should call 911 and get police protection. People should not hesitate to dial 911 because police persons are well trained to handle emergencies to protect civilians. The police will call an ambulance and take the patient to the nearest emergency room if, in their judgment, it is a life-threatening emergency.

If the patient's family can handle the patient, they may take the patient to the emergency room themselves, but it is not generally recommended because many mental patients are unpredictable and there are potential risks for family members who get hurt. I get telephone inquiries about psychiatric emergencies from many Korean-American families. Many times they are reluctant and hesitant to call the police or ambulance out of shame and as a result, they make things worse by missing the right time to help the patient. At times when the police come after the patient calms down momentarily, they conclude that there is no danger and refuse to take emergency measures.

Even if the patient is not violent, if the person expresses the desire to die or commit suicide, you are urged to consult with a psychiatrist by phone, call 911, or take the patient to the nearest hospital emergency room. This is more effective than trying to persuade the patient to change his mind or start an argument with him. In case of an emergency, it is of utmost importance to act swiftly and without being restrained by shame, a desire to "save face," or fear of others' opinions, in order to prevent any harm to the patient or others.

3. Mental Health Warrant

There are situations in which it is not a real psychiatric emergency but the patient is unmanageable at home or poses a potential danger to himself or to others. For this type of patient, the police won't take action to bring the patient to an emergency room because in their judgment the patient poses no danger to anyone. On the other hand, the patient's family will be unsuccessful and will feel helpless because the patient won't admit he has mental problems, refuses to see a psychiatrist on his own and refuses to cooperate with his family who will try to escort him to a psychiatrist or to the psychiatric emergency room. This often happens with chronic psychotic patients. They are clearly disturbed but not agitated nor violent. The symptoms are usually self-limiting and they can easily conceal their symptoms from the police or strangers.

There is a way of helping this type of patient get psychiatric evaluation and treatment. The family member of such a patient should go to the State Supreme Court and speak to the clerk who handles mental health issues. Through this clerk, the family member should file a petition to the Court Judge to issue a "Mental Health Warrant." The judge usually complies with such a petition and issues the warrant. The family then takes the warrant to the police precinct within his jurisdiction. The police will go to the patient's house and take him to the nearest psychiatric emergency room for evaluation by a psychiatrist. If the evaluating psychiatrist finds it necessary to hospitalize the patient (and usually that is the case) then he will do so.

4. Selection of a Psychiatrist

Not every psychiatrist provides all the treatment modalities illustrated above. Usually, however they can provide pharmacotherapy, consultation and some psychotherapy. Other treatment modalities, such as in-depth psychotherapy, psychoanalysis, hypnosis, behavior therapy, electro-convulsive treatment, group therapy, family therapy, marital therapy, treatment for alcohol and drug abuse, treatment of children and so on, can be provided by a psychiatrist who has had additional study and training depending on his preference. Therefore, if a patient is seeking a specific type of treatment he should ask the psychiatrist whether he can provide the type of treatment being sought before making an appointment.

If you are financially burdened, you may go to a clinic. Their fee is usually lower than private psychiatrist's, and they may also have a sliding scale fee according to your income. The drawbacks of a clinic are that you may not be able to find a psychiatrist who speaks your language; you may have some communication problems; and you may not get as much personal attention and care.

5. Important Points to Remember When Receiving Psychiatric Treatment

For most Asians, psychiatry is unfamiliar and their understanding about psychiatric treatment is very limited. As a result, there are many comic episodes owing to these patients. In order to help avoid inconveniences and obstacles; I will illustrate some important points to remember.

A. You Must Make an Appointment in Advance

Almost without exception, most Korean-Americans ask, "Where is your office located?" and "What are your office hours today?" when calling the psychiatrist's office. The hidden intention behind these questions is "I will be there before your office hours are over." Because I know their intention, I give them the location and travel directions while I hastily add that they must make an appointment to see me. Then, they claim that its urgent and request that I see them immediately or today. However, when I ask them what their urgent problems are most of them complain of physical symptoms due to anxiety, depression, or other psychological reasons, for which they have been seeing internists or herb doctors for years. Then for one reason or another it has dawned on

142

them that their problems are psychological, and it becomes an emergency. Or, they become so impatient and insist that I must take care of them immediately! It clearly shows the Korean character of impatience.

Psychiatric practice is different from other specialties. You may go to the primary-care physician or to internists without an appointment, sign up and wait for your turn—provided that you get there within their office hours. It's possible for those doctors to do so because it usually takes less than 15 minutes to take patient's history, to examine him, and write out prescriptions. Besides, there are at least a couple of examination rooms, and the doctor can go from one patient to another depending on the procedure the patient may need. However, the psychiatrist can see you only one at a time giving you undivided attention and spending forty-five minutes to one hour. For these reasons, it is more practical and it makes more sense to make an appointment to see a psychiatrist.

B. You Must Keep the Appointment

Psychiatrists can usually only see one patient at a time and schedule one patient for each hour. If a scheduled patient comes late it can upset the doctor's subsequent appointments because he usually lacks flexibility. Therefore, if you get there 15 minutes late he can't extend your time. Instead, your time has to be cut short. There is no problem getting there earlier, but you have to wait until your appointment time.

For these reasons, you must keep your appointment by all means possible. If, for whatever reasons, you can't keep the appointment, then you must call the doctor and cancel or reschedule your appointment as soon as you decide you can't get to his office. Do this, no matter how many days in advance it is. You should not wait until the last minute to cancel because the doctor should be able to use the slot for other patients who may need him more urgently. For this reason, all psychiatrists strictly adhere to their usual cancellation policy. That is, if you cancel or break your appointment in less than twenty-four hours, you have to pay for the scheduled session anyway. You may think this is unfair, but it is just a courtesy and common sense to respect his time and practice.

C. "Cure My Disease!"

Customarily, when you go to see a doctor, the doctor does everything for you after you tell him your symptoms. He examines you, makes a diagnosis, gives the injections, prescribes drugs, or operates. Patients usually fulfill their responsibility by telling the doctors what their symptoms are and answering the doctor's questions. However, psychiatry is an exception to this general custom because the psychiatrist can't treat you without your co-operation; it is almost impossible for the psychiatrist to treat psychiatric problems without your help. Patients must tell the psychiatrist their symptoms and give answers to his questions, and openly tell him what they feel or think. There is no way for the psychiatrist to find out what you feel or think without talking. Therefore for a speedy recovery, you must cooperate with your psychiatrist in this way. However, because most Asians are unaccustomed to this type of psychotherapy treatment and due to their cultural background in which it is considered to be a merit to be sparsely talkative and hide true, inner feelings there are many bottlenecks in psychiatric treatment.

D. Confidentiality Guaranteed

One of the many reasons that some patients are reluctant to open up their true inner feelings is that they fear their secrets may be spread among the doctors and others. However, in psychiatric practice, legal and ethical confidentiality is guaranteed. The doctor is forbidden to disclose not only contents of the treatment sessions but also anything about the patient without the patient's consent. This includes the mere fact that the patient is in psychiatric treatment. Of the content of treatment, most commonly troublesome issues are that the patient was having an affair with someone without the knowledge of his or her spouse, or perhaps the patient committed a crime or was involved in illegal activities. There are only a few exceptions to the confidentiality code: if there is a risk of a person committing suicide or homicide, the physical or sexual abuse of a minor, or if the patient is involved in litigation and the court subpoenas the patient's records or the psychiatrist. In general, it is not necessary to worry that having a record of psychiatric treatment would interfere with job advancement or finding employment. Therefore for the speedy progress of treatment, patients must feel free to open up whatever they feel inside without reservations.

E. Treatment Fee

As I emphasized before, the main thrust of psychiatric treatment is in psychotherapy, which is verbal therapy. For this reason, patients often do not receive any prescriptions or injections in the course of psychiatric treatment. Rarely, after spending an hour or more in an initial consultation with Korean patients, the patient refuses to pay the fee stating that the psychiatrist did not do anything for him except talk to him. These patients usually have fixed idea that "treatment" involves writing prescriptions or giving injections. But, people must remember that in the United States, most people are paid by the number of hours they work. The axiom "time is money" must be remembered.

F. Health Insurance

Most Asians seem to believe that if they have health insurance, all treatment including psychiatric treatment are fully covered by the insurance. However, this is a big misunderstanding since many insurance companies do not cover psychiatric treatment or cover only small portions of it. It is the same for Medicare and Medicaid. Therefore, many psychiatrists cannot accept health insurance coverage as full payment for their services. In such case, it is a usual practice for patients to pay the full fee to the physician and get a reimbursement from the insurance company for whatever percentage they cover.

However, recently there is a new development in medical insurance coverage. These are H.M.O.'s (Health Maintenance Organizations) and the involvement of Managed Care Companies. Those doctors who participate to these insurance companies must accept their fee as full payment and patient pays a nominal co-payment.

XI

Ways to Make American Life Healthier and Happier

Although we are under a lot of stress to establish a new life in this strange land where no one welcomes us, with little financial means and language problems, there are ways to make American life more rewarding and splendid. However, these ways are not what other people would develop for us but we have to pioneer on our own. It is not an overstatement to say that all immigrants have the potential to lead a successful American life because they already are challenging and progressive by taking the route of immigration despite various unexpected obstacles.

However, having potential is not good enough. In order to have a successful American life, you need guidelines to show the way and you should put them into action in your life. I would like to propose these guidelines based on thirty-five years of life in America, the experience of a psychiatrist treating immigrants, observations of immigrants with keen concern for their mental health, and the expert knowledge of a psychoanalyst who has studied the human mind in depth. The answer is very simple. Just maintain sound mental health! After all, human suffering and happiness depend upon one's mind. American life is not an exception.

There is an historical Korean story to illustrate this point. It is a story of Wonhyo (A.D. 617–686), one of the master monks of Shilla Dynasty of Korea, on his way to China with another master Eusang to further study Buddhism. Shortly before reaching the ferry point to China, severe rain and nightfall prevented them from going forward. They took shelter in a dungeon and decided to spend the night there. Wonhyo groped his hands in the darkness and touched a bowl-like container filled with water. He was so thirsty and exhausted he gulped down the water instantly. It was so refreshing. On waking up in the morning after a good night of sleep, he was able to see the container from which he drank the refreshing water.

It was a human skull!

At the moment of this realization, he became nauseous and began to vomit. However, while vomiting, he became suddenly enlightened that everything was in the play of one's mind. "When I drank the water thinking it was contained in a wooden dipper, it was like nectar. But when I realized it was held in a skull, I considered it dirty and began to vomit. What else could it be but the play of my mind?"

Can you think of any more major enlightenment about essential human nature than this?! Wonhyo felt that he did not need to go to China to further his study after this crucial enlightenment and returned home. Although this is a simple anecdote, this story is a jewel that pierces the essence of human psychology. It is a fundamental truth that the human mind controls our perception of suffering and happiness. Other external factors like wealth, fame, and status are secondary.

In Chapter V of this book, I listed psychological factors that caused mental health problems, such as stress, anxiety, emotional conflict, inferiority feeling, depression, anger, and loneliness. If we could avoid these feelings forever, we could maintain our healthy mental state. But, as long as we are alive, it is impossible to do so. Therefore, the most realistic way to keep mental health sound is by strengthening the ability to handle these feelings well. The best way to achieve this is through the right religious cultivation or psychoanalysis. However, I will address those thoughts in one of my future books. Again I am repeating it, but to keep your mind peaceful and healthy is the key to building a happy American life. The topics I will discuss next are secondary but play important roles in building a happy life.

1. Know Thyself and Be True to Thyself

Whether it's the immigrant life or not, it is a prerequisite to know who and what you are in order to live your life happily with sound mental health. Unfortunately, most people make great efforts to know everything else but the self who is most present and near. They finish their lives complaining about their hard lives without ever understanding themselves. Because you are ultimately responsible for how you respond to all the good and bad things you encounter in life, you must, in order to have a less painful life, at least understand your own personality, what you think, how you feel, and what your strengths and weaknesses are even if you don't have a profound grasp of yourself. We all have a tendency to blame others or external factors when things don't go our way. Of course, this is a psychological defense mechanism to protect us from pain. In order to overcome these mechanisms, you must understand the personalities of others as well as your own. By doing so, one can reduce friction with other people and make sound judgments. Through this understanding, the wisdom to lead American life happily will arise by itself.

2. Know America and Americans

I have heard the best and most fundamental strategy to win a war is to know your self well and to know the other side well. Just knowing either one well is not sufficient to achieve the goal of leading a happy American life. Simply put, one of the major reasons why immigrants are going through so many hardships is because they arrive in the United States without knowing America well. What does the statement, "knowing America" mean?

It, of course, implies knowing the history, culture, geography, climate, people, and so on. But what is more important is to understand the *physiology* of daily living of American people and their society. History, geography, culture, and climate are well described in books, but the physiology of daily living must be picked up through the experience of living in America and bumping into American people directly, or through people who have these experiences. These days, there are many immigrants traveling between the two countries. It's easy to gain information about American life if one desires. One of the major goals of this book is to introduce this *physiology*. There may be some people coming to the United States thinking they will tackle problems as they arise. Well, they may be courageous but they can't avoid mental anguish by tackling problems one by one through trial and error when they must adjust quickly in the early stage of immigration. Some may take these differences lightly thinking that human society is the same no matter where you go. It is true that there may be many similarities between the two countries but there are also many differences as well. Therefore, it is desirable to study America and prepare one's self especially concerning the physiology of American life before landing on this soil in order to adjust quickly and begin enjoying American life as soon as possible. At least, it would be helpful to read Chapter III, titled *Characteristics of American Life,* of this book while preparing for immigration.

For example, most of the poor in America do not have bank accounts and credit cards. This is understandable because most poor people live on governmental monthly welfare support. They must cash their checks immediately upon receipt and spend the money buying food and other basic necessities. Therefore, they buy everything in cash. The reasons that many Korean businessmen run businesses in the indigent areas are because they can manipulate income tax returns with a "cash business" and the poor people who pay in cash seldom come back to the store to exchange or return the items they buy.

Regarding taxes, the taxing system is quite different between our two countries. In Korea, the governmental taxation man visits each business and determines the amount of tax for that business. However, in the United States as we know, it is an honor system. Once a year, by April 15th, each individual must calculate the income and expenses of the household and pay the appropriate tax. Another difference is that in Korea, no matter how big the expense such as buying a house, you must pay the total price in a lump sum all at once. But in the United States, you can buy a house with a bank loan with only a minimum down payment and monthly payments. Therefore, most Americans live life in debt. For this reason, the individual credit in America is of utmost importance. Unless they bring a large sum of cash and deposit it in a bank account to use as a lien, newcomers from other countries will not get any credit in the United States. Good credit can gradually be built up through annual income tax returns, by having a stable salaried job, through records of responsible credit card use, and payment of utility bills. Therefore, even if you earn big cash from a successful business in an indigent area, if you don't deposit the cash income in a bank account regularly and don't file income tax returns, you will not establish a credit record or get credit. Then, you can't buy a house with big cash or borrow money from the bank when you start a business or buy a car.

There is a favorite American joke: "There are two things you can't avoid in life, death and taxes." In Korea, a child will stop crying if someone says, "the tiger is coming!" But, in America, "the I.R.S. is here!" will do the trick. It of course is important to learn the history and culture of America. It is also helpful for your mental health to know useful information such as this.

Another point I would like to make is that in order to live in the United States, it is not sufficient to know only the white culture. It is important to know black people and black culture as well, because many Koreans run businesses in black neighborhoods although there are many other ethnic groups, too. Due to chronic racial discrimination in America, many blacks seem to carry an inferiority complex, resulting in twisted attitudes. They frequently misunderstand others' intentions, are extremely sensitive to any unintentioned slight, and are easily annoyed.

3. You Must Be Clearly Aware of Your Purpose of Immigrating to America

You will have clear directions when you have clear goals, no matter what you undertake. When you decided to immigrate to the United States leaving many loved ones and your hometown behind, you must have had serious resolutions, expectations, and goals. I am sure you didn't immigrate thinking vaguely that you want "to have a better life," or "I'll go because everyone else is going." If you want to have a better life, it should be clear to you what a better life actually is. Because Korea now is economically stronger and wealthier, it is more essential to have a clear purpose for immigration. For some, a better life may mean living away from severe environmental pollution; or having better opportunities for education of their children; or pursuing higher education that is unavailable in Korea. For others it means making a lot of money; or having a retirement in America with a fortune he made in Korea; or living away from the annoyance of in-laws; or, living in a country where there is more political freedom away from dictatorship or a harsh military government; or leading an artistic life utilizing one's creativity thoroughly; or introducing and spreading Asian cultures in United States. One's goals can vary depending on the purpose of immigration, but by having a clear purpose, he can establish the direction of his American life, avoid the pain of indecisiveness or fluctuation, and enjoy American life better.

4. Learn Spoken English

There are differences between the written and spoken word in any language. Unless you are born in the United States, you can't expect to speak English perfectly. However, as long as you are living in United States, you need to know daily spoken English to be able to access social and government agencies and banks. Of course, it will help you in running your business too. As mentioned before, everyday English is usually composed of easy words. But, there are often so many different usages for a single word; you should never try to take a guess of the meaning of idioms composed of simple and easy words because often these are beyond your guesswork. English education in Korea tends to teach difficult words, but everyday English is made of easy words and simple sentences. It may be true to some extent that you can get by without knowing and speaking English in big cities like New York and Los Angeles where there are many ethnic immigrants. However, you can't find everything from Korea in America and the social structure between the two countries is so different that you can't live as if you are in Korea while actually living in America. I don't have to tell you that whoever has the better command of the language of the society you are living in will be more successful! Therefore, it can't be overemphasized to study English hard for better adjustment and mental health. Studying English in America should be much easier than studying in Korea because everybody uses English here in America.

5. Understand the American Culture Thoroughly

Even in the same ethnic group, there are unique traditions and cultures in every household. If, for example, the daughter-in-law does not understand, accept, or adjust to the tradition and culture of her husband's household, she will develop friction with her in-laws and family problems will develop. Much more so when you are living in a huge and strange country, you'll have hard time adjusting if you don't know the culture and tradition and do not digest it. First of all, you must understand both Korean and American culture well, grasp the differences and similarities, and adjust appropriately. There is no superior or inferior culture. However, it is necessary to have an open mind to accept and discard whatever is required for the sake of your own mental health. This is also important because it will affect the attitude of the second generation Korean-Americans. There are some extreme people who reject anything Korean and try to behave as born Americans, and vice versa, but both groups are doomed to invite unhappiness.

For example, in Korea it is acceptable to eat dog meat, but in America even abusing dogs is absolutely unacceptable. However, there is no need to make judgments as to which is good or bad. Simply put, there is no need to insist stubbornly that you must eat dog meat when you come to live in America. Another example on a positive note is that, in Korea there is the beautiful custom of children bowing to their parents and elders on New Year's Day to show respect and receive words of encouragement. However, there is no reason not to observe this lovely custom just because Americans do not have similar customs. Unless you understand the differences between the customs and handle them appropriately, you may get into trouble unnecessarily. As I mentioned before and as occasionally reported in Korean newspapers, some Korean adults have been arrested for fondling the penis of a child on charges of sexual abuse of children. Of course in Korea, it is an accepted custom for an adult to fondle a child's penis as a way of saying they are "cute." But in the United States, there is no such custom and this behavior will never be accepted. You can avoid this kind of disastrous trouble and adjust more quickly by knowing the American culture well.

6. Realize That Money and Material Wealth Are *Not* the Most Important Goals

During my discussion of American values in the previous chapter, I mentioned that the United States is a country where materialism has flourished. That is, it is a land where money wields its power most blatantly. So, there is an abundance of goods and services you can buy with money as well as many dazzling luxurious goods. As a result people easily place money and material assets high on their criteria of values. In fact, this trend is a chronic malady of America.

In contrast, morality flourished more highly than materialism in the Orient. However, it is lamentable to see many Korean-Americans turning to a level of materialism that makes Americans pale. It is understandable that the goal of many Koreans who immigrate to the United states is financial improvement, but they behave as if making money is the most important goal in life. This deception must be tamed for the sake of sound mental and physical health. Of course, we all need money to live on. But, when you run to the extreme to make money by any means and incur many sacrifices without hesitation for yourself and others, you will invite unhappiness and damage your mental health. There may be many reasons for this attitude. Many Koreans engage in businesses in which little skill is required, but the work is physically exhausting. Also, many open businesses in dangerous, indigent areas where they can make cash income quickly. When they begin working in the United States, there is no such distinction between a noble or mean occupation, but the trouble begins when those engaged in a so-called mean occupation begin to earn some money and life becomes somewhat financially comfortable. They begin to feel that their pride is injured and lament that their job is menial while complaining, "I am highly educated and had a highly respected position in Korea!" Also, it is a well-known fact that many Korean-owned stores are robbed at gunpoint and at times the owners are killed.

People who run around with the utmost goal of making a fortune sacrifice many more valuable things in life. They push these valuable treasures aside because they are invisible and intangible. For example, in a family where husband and wife run around to make money fast, the happiness of their children is sacrificed; their schoolwork will become poor, there will be a setback in healthy development of their character, at times, they'll become "problem children" and inflict unhappiness on the whole family. The next things that may be sacrificed are their pride, self-respect and other important elements that would enrich their lives, such as physical exercise, traveling, appreciation of music and art, reading, writing, and other hobbies. When you sacrifice these things, you reduce your self-esteem, worsen your discontent about yourself, and deepen your unhappy feelings.

To overcome these feelings, some of the unsuccessful immigrants seek positions of leadership. They try to become president of one of many Korean-American associations or organizations, or the elder of a Korean church while spending hard earned money in order to restore a damaged self-esteem, overcome feelings of inferiority and escape nihilism. Of course, this is all pursued unconsciously. As a result, in the Korean-American community, those who became rich claim to be the leaders and the communities support these people rather than those with respectable character and high education. To avoid any misunderstanding of my statement, let me state that among these financially successful people, there are ones with respectful characters, advanced educations and a sincere desire to serve the community.

It is a fact in the Korean-American community that there is a vicious circle due to materialism and its side effects. This trend created an atmosphere in the Korean-American community of trying to present one's wealth as proof of personal success or pride. This instigates competition among Korean-Americans to show off to others that they own luxury cars, gorgeous houses and expensive furniture, which increases their mental conflict, and adds unnecessary stress.

We all know that money alone won't make us happy. The element of true happiness lies in the invisible, intangible things that bring genuine satisfaction with one's self. There-fore, for the sake of a healthy and happy American life, one should not let money making be the goal of life. It should be only one of the means for a happy life. Because there is strong tendency toward money worshipping in America where we immigrated thinking it would be a better place to live, we can easily become contaminated by this trend. However, we should take great care not to unconditionally accept and iden-tify with this philosophy of money worshipping because it is a serious social malady that tramples over human dignity. The society is structured in such a way that if you make less money you can get by and if it's the opposite, you are com-pelled to spend excessively. If you become addicted to money, you won't be happy no matter how much money you make. Moneymaking will become a pleasureless, blind behavior. There is no rule that the poor will always be poor, or that the rich will remain rich. So, it will be better for the sake of your mental health not to be obsessed with money or material possession or to invest too much of your pride in it.

7. Be Patient

Many Americans who have had long associations with Koreans often say in describing the Korean character that they are too straightforward, too hasty, and impatient. I am a Korean who did not have any opportunities to compare us with other ethnic groups while living in Korea and was not aware of these characteristics. But, after living in the United States and observing various people for 35 years, I can safely say these descriptions are very accurate.

These characteristics are observed most prominently in the attitudes of earning a living. I know of no other ethnic group that continually works so hard. This is seen most often among newly arrived Koreans. Of course, the underlying intention is to make money fast and live proudly. So, we frequently see husband and wife working and running around day and night. However, the damage stemming from this hasty and impatient behavior is enormous. As stated before, they may irrevocably damage their physical health; die ironically from a heart attack or stroke while driving the new luxury car they just bought; be robbed or killed by thieves; ruin their family life; or raise children who create problems at school and outside the home. They often end up regretting their impatient money-making behavior. In America, no one starves to death if they are diligent. So, it is desirable to proceed patiently and consistently after determining which priorities are most important.

Many Americans do not move hastily. Therefore, new immigrants complain that they feel irritated. In Korea all services are carried out instantly; whereas in America, most stores close early, many businesses are closed on Sundays, and any order placed often takes long time for a response. Lately in America, more stores and businesses remain open late in the evening, but it still is no comparison to Korea.

The impatience of Koreans is well exhibited in their attitudes toward psychiatric treatment. As mentioned, occasionally some patients walk in without appointments and ask to be seen immediately. Frequently, many patients call and just ask where my office is located or what are my office hours, implying that they want to come in that day. Some even say they will come to see me "right now." When I ask whether it's a medical emergency, the answer is usually no but they still want to be taken care of right away. When I ask the person to make an appointment, they become very disappointed.

When they start treatment, they often complain if their problem isn't cured right away. Most psychiatric treatment takes time. For some illnesses, lifetime treatment is necessary. There is a Korean proverb that says, "Even a cow's horn should be extracted instantly!" This means that if you do anything, do it quickly.

Such proverbs illustrate the ethnic characteristic derived from Confucian influences. I believe, prior to Confucianism, while people were living under the influence of Buddhism, they were living in a more relaxed state. The reason being that in Buddhist teachings, there is no demand for perfectionism or ritualistic framing as in Confucianism. Since the perfectionist cannot tolerate anything less than perfect, he must do the things that have to be done, or correct what has to be corrected in haste in order to eliminate anxiety.

However, with human matters and world matters, especially in adjusting to this country, there are so many things you have no control over. So, if you handle things patiently and step-by-step without worry, you will avoid any trouble, things will go smoothly, and you can lead your life soundly with a sound mind. The Japanese saying, "If you are in a hurry, go around!" means that if you take a short cut in order to get there fast, you will get into trouble and end up getting there late. What a golden maxim that is so helpful in everyday living.

8. Maintain an Optimistic Attitude

If you are impatient, you can't be optimistic. Everything will go more smoothly if you are optimistic. You're apt to suffer less and find more pleasure in your life if you are optimistic. On the other hand, if you assume a pessimistic attitude, things can easily go wrong and pleasurable activities will become a chore. I am sure everyone experiences stuffy and frustrating feelings by being with a pessimistic person.

Of course, I don't mean you should be optimistic without action; blind optimism that ignores reality is rather pathological and harmful. But, assuming an optimistic attitude after doing everything realistically possible is healthy; you will sleep better, eat well, alleviate mental agony, and lead a brighter life. Whether you are optimistic or pessimistic will depend on your attitude of looking at the same matter. *You* determine your attitude, not the external matter. To quote the popular example, it's a question of "whether the glass is half empty or half full." You are free to choose either, but for the same price it is more helpful to be optimistic for your mental well-being.

I am sure many have heard this anecdote. There was a mother who had two sons: one was a shoe salesman and the other sold umbrellas. When it rained, she worried about the son who sold shoes because he might not sell enough shoes. When the sun shone, she worried for the same reason about the son who sold umbrellas. So, not a day passed for this mother without worries, complaints, and misery. The woman next door had been watching this pitiful woman for years and finally could not take it anymore. So, one day, she spoke to this hopeless woman.

"Look, dear, I can't stand you anymore! When it rains, your younger son will sell more umbrellas, when it shines, your older son will sell more shoes. So, you can be happy every day, can't you?" Fortunately, the mother was not stupid. It enlightened her and she lived happily everyday thereafter. In fact, happiness is like flipping one's hand and entirely up to how one looks at life.

Of course, there are many things that will make you feel nervous and frustrated after immigrating to America. But, things won't become any better simply because you assume a pessimistic attitude, and things won't become spoiled simply because you are optimistic. If anything, things usually go better when they are handled with an optimistic attitude. It is better for mental health to make your best effort and wait for the outcome.

9. Acculturate Actively

Previously, I defined *acculturation* as the process of adjusting one's self to the given cultural environment harmoniously. It sounds very passive. For example, in the past, when different ethnic groups with different cultural backgrounds immigrated to the United States (mostly whites), they became assimilated to American culture as if melting away in a big cauldron and that was considered the best way to adjust to American culture. However, for Asians, the American cultural environment does not provide entirely favorable conditions. Imagine the old men with inflexible brain function, trying to learn English and trying to eat American foods in order to adjust to this culture. Well, it certainly will be counterproductive, painful, and more difficult to adjust to American life. In fact, acculturation does not mean external change alone; the change of inner thinking process is more fundamental. Acculturation should not be adjustment confined to the given conditions; it include adjustment by actively changing the given environment to better suit it for one's self.

When I first came to United States in 1964, there were few Asians here and I was busy learning American life and imitating Americans. It never occurred to me to change the American way of life. To live on the land where no one welcomed me, I didn't have the sense that I belonged here. I became self-conscious and concerned with what Americans might think of me. However, things are different now. Because the history of Korean immigration is over 30 years now and the number of Korean immigrants has grown, we should actively try to change the environment to suit our needs.

Koreans are already involved in active adjustment. It started with successfully convincing the government to provide the test for driver's licenses in Korean. Also, the numbers of government documents written in Korean are increasing. It may be for the sake of business, but there are more Korean bank tellers in the Korean community and there are Korean overseas telephone operators. The stores run by Korean immigrants, especially fruits-and-vegetable stores, are much cleaner and more tastefully arranged; so much so that everybody likes them. At one of the Ivy League colleges, Yale University, students took the initiative to request the school administration to teach the Korean language and history several years ago and these courses have been in the curriculum ever since. Other American colleges are following suit. These are a few examples that illustrate how Koreans can be progressive, active, and creative. All immigrants should maintain these active attitudes and lead American life into a positive direction.

10. Realize That Korean-Americans Are *Not* a Minority

The term *minority* can be defined as the ethnic group less in number and other than the ruling ethnic group of the society in which they belong. According to this definition, Koreans living in America are clearly a minority group. Because minorities generally have a lower socio-economic status, the American government protects their interests by laws in order to promote their growth. For example, there are laws to prevent discrimination against minorities buying a house or renting an apartment. There are the laws to prevent discrimination against minorities in employment; such as, the number of minorities on the job should be proportional to the composition of the community where the job is located and there is a quota of minority students assigned to each college. Up until 20 years ago, Asians were beneficiaries of these minority benefits. However, I am not certain when it began, but Asians are excluded from these minority benefits, although racial discrimination is still there to a lesser degree. Sometime ago, it was publicized in the major newspapers that the most prestigious universities in the nation now have a hidden quota system by which not to exceed the admission of Asian students that is the opposite of the official quota system to admit more minorities. The reason being that if they accept students according to their grades, there will be far more Asian students admitted than whites and other races due to the fact that there are so many excellent Asian students. Also, the average annual income of Asians is higher than that of whites, so that social welfare benefits also seem to be curtailed for Asian Americans.

For these reasons, the so-called minority status is primarily limited to blacks and Latinos although they outnumber Asians. So, it is now time to redefine the term *minority*. That is, being less in number alone is not sufficient, but at the same time it should include lower education and poor social advancement within a racial group. Therefore, the Asian translation of minority must be changed too because it literally means "fewer number" only. Accordingly, Asian immigrants living in America must discard the thinking that they are minorities and should be proud of being Asian.

11. Be Proud of Being a Korean

People can enjoy their lives fully when they are proud of, are happy with, and dignify themselves. Being proud means having trust in one's values and ability while dignity stands for the mind with self-respect. It is necessary to have something to believe in and to trust in order to have pride and dignity.

While living in Korea, you had pride and dignity with your good school background, good family background, affluent assets, good job, political power, etc., but once you immigrated to the United States things were quite different. The reasons for the difference being that these things do not have such might in America, and in addition, you experienced an inferiority complex as an ethnic group. Of course, in this capitalistic society, wealth may bring you some pride, but there are too many millionaires for you to compete with. Many regain their personal pride and dignity by high academics and professional achievements. But, it will take time to restore ethnic and racial pride. One of the main reasons is, as mentioned earlier, the fact that you can hardly have the sense of being the host of this land. Leaving our homeland for a better life indirectly expresses that this country is superior to our native country, which in itself creates an ethnic inferiority complex. In addition, the sense of white supremacy is widespread both covertly and overtly here in United States. This in turn creates a racial inferiority complex due inevitably to our different appearance and skin color. Also, we can fall into cultural inferiority as well. As stated earlier, there are no other emotions that kill human spirit, bring down the energy for activity, and stunt the growth so much as inferiority complex. Especially for immigrants, it contributes to a delay in acculturation and interferes with the building of a happy American life. For the purpose of overcoming an inferiority complex, some totally reject all that is American and insist on only that which is Korean or vice versa. Occasionally, I meet some Korean immigrants who anglicize their names, marry a white mate, speak only English, and cut social ties with Korean-Americans. I think it's futile and only a self-deception. Who will accept him as white, or entirely American? These people should realize that they are digging graveyards of disappointment and despair into which they will fall. The pride of these extreme people by insisting on *only* Korean or only American is a blind and morbid attitude. Then, what are the things we can hold to have true pride and dignity?

A. Be Proud of Your Roots

It's better to be proud of your Korean roots because you can't hide the fact that you are Asians. Koreans deserve to be proud of their country and their people because Korea now has joined the ranks of the developed countries by making such wonderful economic, political, and cultural progress. Even if Korea is still a developing country, as it was thirty years ago, we still should be proud of our roots. People respect those who can stand proudly as they are, more than those who look timid and as if they feel inferior. We should feel proud of the fact that there is a country we can go back to if we fail to adjust to American life.

One day, several years ago, a black patient came to see me and became annoyed because I refused to prescribe the habit-forming drug he wanted. He shouted at me, "You f—ing Yellow, why don't you go back to your country!"

I am a patient man but I was annoyed with his racial remark and told him, "Good, there is a country I can go back to if I want, but do you have such a country?!"

I said it because I was well aware of the racial discrimination the blacks have to bear. He looked shocked, lost for words to say and quietly walked out. I felt fortunate that there is a country I can go back to if I could not bear the sorrow of racial discrimination, and felt sorry for stabbing the black man in his most weak point.

Then, what about the first generation born in America? Can they go back to Korea like their parents? And, what about the immigrant generation, and those Korean-born children who came to United States with their parents? Must they live in America like the blacks, thinking this is their mother country in spite of the racial discrimination they suffer? I don't have any clear answer to these questions. However, the roots of the Koreans who immigrated are Korean even though they are branching out in this country. They should value and cherish their Korean roots in order to have the dignity essential to co-exist in peace and live proudly in this multi-racial nation. Likewise, our children born in America must embrace and value their Korean roots in order to have the pride and dignity needed to have the self-confidence to live in American society as well as boost the status of Korean-Americans here in the United States. Through these interactions, their sense of being the host of this land will solidify, too. In other words, minorities can adjust and acculturate better when they have a strong sense and pride of their original roots.

B. Be Proud of Your Native Culture

The next thing you can trust in and hold out is Korean traditional culture. Regardless of origin, all cultures are equal in value. Although the United States is the strongest country in the world, that does not make the American culture superior to other cultures. Rather, in the sense that its history is much shorter, the American culture is behind Korean culture. In fact, contemporary American culture is typically morally decayed and morbid in thought. Nevertheless, all other countries in the world import American culture without screening, and imitate it unconditionally, turning the entire world morbid.

Until the 1950s Americans expected and wanted all immigrants to discard their native culture and assimilate completely into American culture. Of course, that was not a problem for white immigrants from Europe. However, as many different races and ethnic groups started to enter this country this has become impossible. Also, people realized that these immigrants can contribute more to American society and its progress when their ethnic prides are enhanced. As a result, most Americans now accept cultural diversity and encourage it. American attitudes have gone from the old idea of the "melting pot" to that of a "salad bowl." For this reason, there are many different traditional cultural activities unique to different ethnic groups. In New York alone, every year there is a Korean Parade, an Asian Festival, "Choo-Suk" (August Moon or Thanksgiving) feast, etc. In addition, there are many small cultural activities. These happenings are a desirable and welcoming development, because through these activities, Korean-Americans can solidify their "root sense," enhance their pride and dignity, and adjust to American life better.

Of course, it is also desirable for immigrants to know Western culture well because they came to live in America. However, it is not acceptable to reject the traditional Korean culture, art, and tradition that belong to you, your ancestors, and your offspring forever. If you do, your behavior may be considered toadyism, a symptom of ethnic neurosis and personal inferiority complex. That would be going against American life and even Americans would not like such behavior.

C. Double Responsibility

Korean immigrants bear the double burden of mastering Korean, as well as American, culture. Due to a misguided educational system, I went through my childhood listening primarily to Western music and learning Western art history. I was told those are the classics of music and art. I never had even a single session at school about traditional Korean music and Oriental painting. What a shame! Even now, whenever I remember this experience, I turn red with anger. Now, it is welcome news to hear that in Korea they begin teaching traditional Korean music and dance in elementary school. Not too long ago, I heard from an Indian doctor that since childhood, they learned only traditional Indian music and art as the classics and were never told that Western music and art are the classics. Of course, this is a limited example, but it clearly shows a lack or poverty of national identity of some Koreans regardless any excuses they may offer.

After coming to the United States, I happened to come across some traditional Korean music. Once I indulged myself in traditional Korean music, dance, painting, and art culture, I was shocked to realize their excellent quality, how they warmed my heart, and how well they hit home. Of course, I also enjoy Western art but I could not avoid feeling something foreign there. With traditional Korean art, I experienced such a joy, ecstasy and empathy. Beside art, I felt such a pride after studying Oriental thoughts of Confucianism, Buddhism, and Taoism in realizing the depth of truth and unparalleled humanism that the Western philosophy and religion could hardly contain. I do not feel the need to elaborate the strengths of Western culture here because we are already familiar with them.

As I mentioned above, there are many other cultural elements that will bring you pride and dignity as a Korean,

169

such as language and interdependent, humane, family-centered tradition. It can't be overemphasized that Korean-Americans must study traditional Korean culture more diligently than when they were living in Korea, introduce their culture to other ethnic groups, participate more actively to Korean cultural activities, and live with a heightened sense of ethnic pride and dignity. Of course, the same goes for those Korean-American children born in this country.

In conclusion, it will be helpful for sound mental health for the immigrant generation to become familiar with the Western and American culture and to live with the feeling that we are model Koreans living in America. It is equally important for the second and third generation to live with the feeling that we are model Americans with Korean roots.

12. Create a New "Korean-American Culture"

If you say the West is the center of materialistic civilization, the East may be called that of moral civilization. The United States is a country where materialism has flourished in its extreme form. Unfortunately, all other countries in the world are struggling to catch up with American materialism. Thus, we see them importing American degenerate and pathological by-products without any scrutiny and imitating their example. Examples are, hedonism, drug abuse, moral decay, murder, sex crime, destruction of the family, the attitude of any means are justifiable to make money, etc. The strengths of materialism are that there are plenty of goods and a comfortable life due to the mechanical civilizations. The weaknesses of materialism are that it destroys nature and human dignity is pushed away.

Although there may be disadvantages in materialistic deficiencies and inconvenience in a life where spiritual civilization is more advanced, there are merits to having esteem of nature and respecting humans and humanism over material-ism. Which is more important of the two will vary according to each individual, but unfortunately in this modern era material civilization is prevailing over moral civilization. Since Korea, known as the most courteous country in the East and where Confucianism is most respected in the world, joined the ranks of the capitalistic countries, there has been a wide spread of immorality and corruption that would make Americans pale. Although I feel quite uncomfortable about these changes, there still are more value systems of Eastern morals in Korea than in America. I hope that Korean-Americans will become a model and leader toward elevating human dignity higher in American society. The history of mass Korean immigration spans over 30 years and the number of Korean-Americans in the United States is now over a million. Since the superiority of Koreans has been proven throughout the world, it's now time to play a leader's role rather than passively accepting and imitating whatever is American.

The method lies in the creation of new "Korean-American culture" that combines the strengths of both American materialism and Eastern morality. However, there is no way to clearly predict what kind of shape it will take because this is a new culture evolving and being developed by Korean-Americans. I can only say that this should be a culture in which human desire for material wealth is not rejected and the convenience of life brought by machine civilization is enjoyed while respecting humanism and human dignity based on morality. This may be comparable to the Romanticism movement in 18th-century Europe, and may be called the "Second Romanticism" movement that advocates returning to "nature" by freeing human beings from the machine civilization. This is the third culture I mentioned in Chapter III, "Characteristics of American Life and the Problems that Immigrants Experience."

13. You Must Become Korean-Americans in a True Sense

A. What Is Korean-American?

In American society, Korean immigrants are called Korean-Americans or we call ourselves as such. Regardless of whether you are an immigrant or the children of immigrants, you are called "Asian-Americans." As long as you look Asian whether Chinese-American, Japanese-American, Korean-American, Indian-American, etc., you are a hyphenated American. Among the whites that came from Europe, some call themselves at times as Irish-Americans, Italian-American, French-American, etc., but other people don't call them hyphenated. In other words, people like to use this hyphenated name mostly for non-white groups. This is more proof of racial discrimination toward non-white ethnic groups because of a prevailing attitude of white supremacy by whites, the majority group.

Therefore, Koreans who could never become white no matter what they do would never be called simply "Americans" unless there was a revolutionary change in America, and this habit of being called "Korean-Americans" will continue for some time. However, if Korean-Americans create an outstanding Korean-American culture and become models and leaders to clean up and correct this morally decaying American society, then this hyphenated title of "Korean-American" would become the symbol of enhancing their personal and ethnic pride. In other words, in this American society where many different ethnic groups co-exist and are called the "salad bowl," we should not be satisfied to exist as a vegetable piece within in it, but should become the dressing that determines the taste of the salad. My thoughts and proposals such as these are not just dreams. In 1991, the Education Department of the State of New York organized a

Special Educational Committee and asserted that in the process of teaching history and social studies at schools, they should teach the influence of minority cultures to American history and society. That is, they should break from white- and European-centered education. If this kind of awakening among Americans continues spreading, there will soon be the day when a new Korean-American culture is developed and accepted. With this newly created culture, Korean-Americans will play a leadership role and soon we all will live with the sense of being the host of this land and not unwelcome travelers. When we lead the American life with this type of attitude, we will have pride and dignity, and will have happier lives.

B. A Definition of True Korean-Americans

In broad sense, everyone with Korean roots and living in America can be called Korean-American, whether you are an immigrant or the offspring of an immigrant. However, this broad definition is meaningless because it does not give us any clear sense of ethnic identity. The hyphenated term *Korean-American* should represent an identity and we need to have a clear identity to know how to behave in the society we live. In our case, shall we behave like an American or like a Korean? For now, we can't behave as an American because we are not accepted fully as such. On the other hand, we can't behave as all Korean because we are living in America. Therefore, we coined the term *Korean-American* in order to identify ourselves as a separate entity. In order to give us a sense of direction and identity, I propose the true definition of Korean-American as "a person with a Korean background who is a respectable Korean on one hand and, at the same time, a respectable American on the other, who is creating a respectable Korean-American culture." I am sure this will

173

give us a clear direction as to how we should behave in this world. In order to become a model Korean-American in the true sense, we have to make great efforts to achieve the goal because there is double the responsibility trying to be both than to become only one or the other. When we can feel and present ourselves as Korean-American in the true sense, we will keep sound mental health and life will become happier in America.

I have proposed a few ways of making American life healthier and happier, but there are many other factors, too. In conclusion, I would like to emphasize that the most important factor of all is maintaining a healthy mind or mental status. Therefore, it can't be over-emphasized to get treatment immediately when mental or emotional problems develop. Also, lead your life so as to prevent mental problems from developing. In other words, the secret of leading a happy American life is keeping a healthy and peaceful mind. This is the most important factor for making one's entire life meaningful and happy as well.

Closing Words

While I was proofreading the original Korean version of this book, the race riots erupted in Los Angeles, California. The riots were sparked when four white policemen who were accused of beating a black man named Rodney King were indicted but were released as being innocent after the trial. But the serious problem was that the victims of the riot were not members of the white community but the Korean community. Many Korean stores were destroyed and set on fire.

When analyzed, everything this book deals with, such as characteristics and physiology of American society and how hard it is for Koreans to adjust to American life, is well illustrated in the race riots of Los Angeles. That is, the serious racial problems of this capitalistic country, problems of social advocacy, social classification based on an individual's wealth, the blindness of efforts to maintain social order exclusively by law, poor compliance with the law, mistrust of the government, the anarchistic world of firearms, etc.

Also, we can see the characteristic impatience of Koreans and their exclusive and contemptuous attitude toward blacks, conflicts brought on by certain adventurous and progressive behaviors, and the resulting big sacrifice of Korean life and property. Of course, there are some blacks who are uneducated and poor who steal. But, this is not unique to the black community and we must not fear them, guard ourselves against them, or mistreat them unconditionally. After all, they too are Americans and in order to live in America, we must find harmony with them.

America is no longer the land of whites alone. There are many other races and ethnic groups living together now. Therefore, our efforts must not be limited solely to understanding whites and white culture. We should try to understand other ethnic groups, especially blacks, their culture and their psychology as well. We must figure out why the Korean-American community became the target of black riots while excluding the white community when it erupted because of the mistreatment of a black man by whites.

I hope the readers of this book have gained much wisdom in understanding America, in adjusting well to American society actualizing American dreams, and in leading healthy and happy American lives.

I would like to acknowledge and express my sincere gratitude to the members of The Institute for Korean-American Culture and to those who encouraged me to write an English version of this book for their children.